Tuned Percussion/Counter Melody/Keyboard

Leckie & Leckie

COUNTER
melody

Bumper Pack

complete class music

new music for group performance

John Montgomery

Leckie & Leckie's original music book containing
30 progressive pieces arranged for group performance

Leckie & Leckie

All compositions written and arranged by John Montgomery
Computer sequencing and scoring by Andrew Montgomery
Drumkit arrangements by Allan Brown
Guitar on Class Music CD played by Paul Devery
Edited by Sheila Cochrane
Thanks to Brian Carty, Emily Dewhurst, Bruce Ryan and Norman Stewart

ISBN 1-898890-16-1

Published by
Leckie & Leckie Ltd
8 Whitehill Terrace
St Andrews
Scotland KY16 8RN
tel: 01334 475656
fax: 01334 477392
email: hq@leckieandleckie.com
web: www.leckieandleckie.com

A CIP Catalogue record for this publication is available from the British Library.

® Leckie & Leckie is a registered trademark.

INVESTOR IN PEOPLE Leckie & Leckie Ltd achieved the Investors in People Standard in 1999.

New Music for Schools

**30 progressive pieces
arranged for group performance
featuring**

Guitar (Acoustic or Electric) / Melody
Guitar Tab Melody
<u>Tuned Percussion</u>
<u>Counter Melody</u>
B flat Melody
B flat Counter Melody
Bass Guitar
Drum Kit / Untuned Percussion
<u>Keyboard/Single Finger Chords</u>
Piano

all music also available on CD
(see page 6 and back cover)

contents

introduction

Complete Class Music is a new and exciting book containing 30 original pieces for group performing.

It features progressive music for 'classroom' and orchestral instruments and is intended for the early years of secondary education leading to preparation for GCSE and Standard Grade music performances.

The flexible arrangements and layout allow endless possibilities for performing at different levels and a unique opportunity for students to play in varying group/class ensembles.

Complete Class Music features the following parts:

- Guitar (Acoustic or Electric)/Melody

- Guitar Tab Melody

- Tuned Percussion

- Counter Melody

- B flat Melody

- B flat Counter Melody

- Bass Guitar

- Drum Kit/Untuned Percussion

- Keyboard/Single Finger Chords

- Piano

Every piece in *Complete Class Music* has been carefully composed to help you make steady progress in your playing.

Complete Class Music is not a tutor book. Please consult with your teacher for advice on posture, musicianship and performance. Experiment with tempo, repeats, leaving parts out, expression, etc, to suit your group's and your own performance needs.

Enjoy using this book while making good progress with your instrumental work in both solo and group performance.

John Montgomery

PS
Leckie & Leckie has also published *Class Music Guitar Melody Book*, containing a book of the 30 Class Music melody parts taken from *Complete Class Music*, and the accompanying *Class Music* CD. The *Class Music* CD is designed for you to play along with your live performances. By adjusting the balance control on your stereo, you can listen to the full arrangement, to the melody part only or to the backing tracks alone.

group sizes for performance

1. A Full Class

A typical group of 20 players could be:

either 8 guitars/
melody (depending on
melody instruments) or
1 or 2 electric guitars
4 glocks/metallaphones
1 bass guitar
1 keyboard
1 drumkit (brushes
should be considered in
many pieces)
2 B flat players (eg
clarinet)
2 counter melody (eg
xylophone/keyboard)
1 piano

2. Group Ensemble

Where groups can play in separate rehearsal areas, electric guitar can be used as a solo melody instrument.

In this case, a typical group of 8 players could be:

1 electric guitar/melody
1 bass guitar
1 drumkit (sticks)
1 keyboard
1 piano
1 B flat instrument (eg trumpet)
1 counter melody (eg flute)
1 tuned percussion (eg glock/marimba)

3. Smaller Groups

A typical group of five players could be:

2 recorders
1 keyboard
1 bass
1 guitar chords

You may wish to play as a solo or practise for future group performance, or indeed use the melody part with chords for keyboard study.

There are endless combinations and schools will adapt to situations which suit them. The above are only suggestions of groupings you may wish to consider.

guide to levels

Here is a table with the suggested levels of difficulty of the pieces. These levels are an approximate guide. You should always check levels with your teacher when you are preparing for your exams.

Pre-level 1
Preparation for level 1

Level 1
GCSE level 1 (easy)
Standard Grade Foundation Level
SQA Access 3
Preparation for Schools of Music Grade 1

Level 2
GCSE level 2 (less easy)
Standard Grade General Level
SQA Intermediate 1
Schools of Music Grades 1/2

Level 3
GCSE level 3 (moderate)
Standard Grade Credit Level
SQA Intermediate 2
Schools of Music Grades 2/3

Level 4
GCSE level 4 (difficult)
SQA Higher
Schools of Music Grades 3/4

helpful information

Tuned Percussion

Decide what tuned percussion instruments are most suitable. This will depend on three main factors:

1. Which instruments are available in your school.
2. What type of sound suits the particular piece you are playing.
3. What other instruments are playing in your group.

The *Class Music* CD features mainly glockenspiel/metallaphones and the occasional use of xylophone and marimba. In most pieces use metal surface keys to promote a degree of sustaining sound.

Keyboards

No particular voicings have been suggested due to the great variation of keyboard instruments currently being used in schools and at home. Consider using sustained sounds (eg 'strings') for most of the pieces. Experiment with the many different moods suggested by the music and listen to the *Class Music* CD for ideas.

Counter Melody

These parts have been written to suit all manner of 'classroom' and orchestral instruments (e.g. recorder, tuned percussion, oboe and flute) You can employ other instruments you are using for 'melody' purposes. The *Class Music* CD offers various combinations of counter melody options.

main recorder finger positions

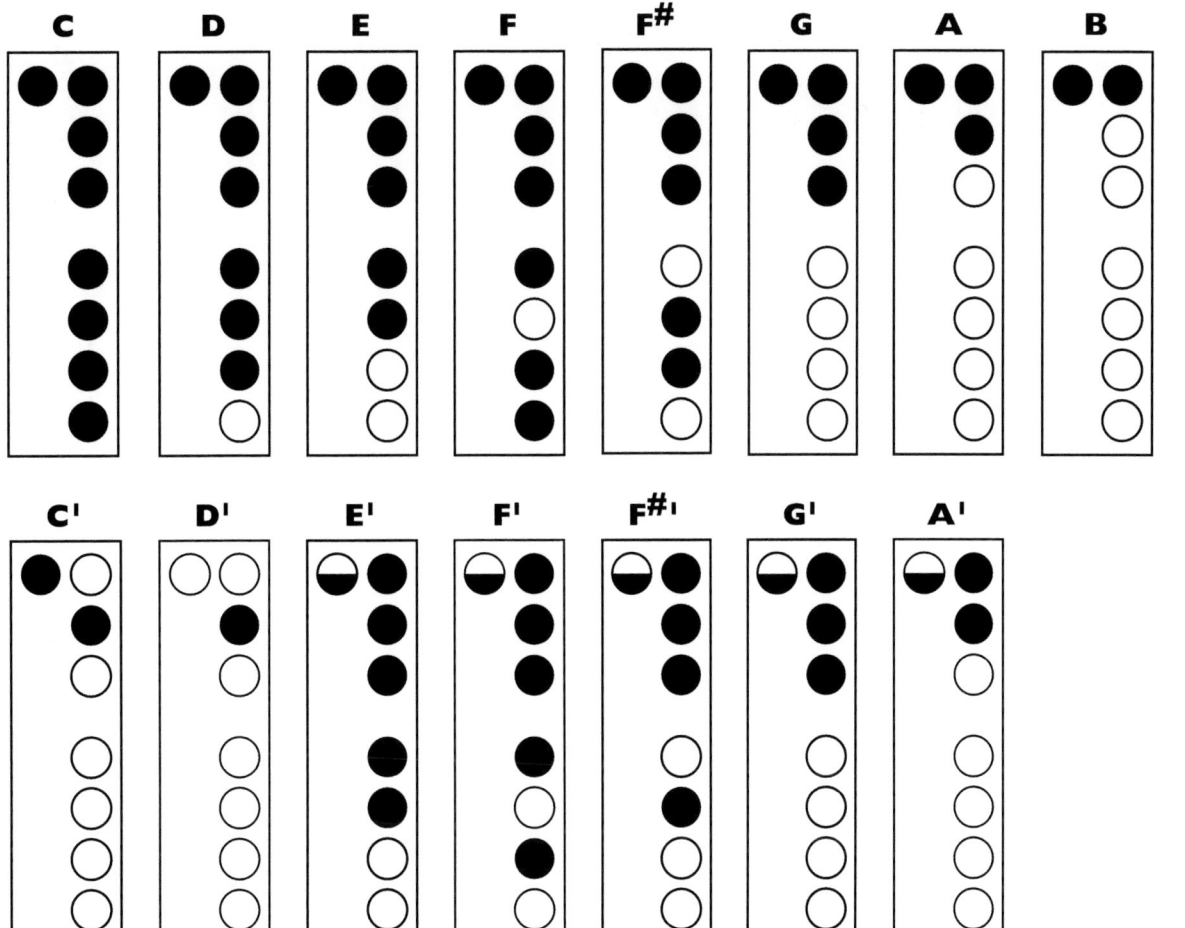

Recorder notes in order of finger positions

C D E F F# G A B C' D' E' F' F#' G' A'

class music bumper pack
keyboard, counter melody and tuned percussion

1. Starting Out

Moderately 118

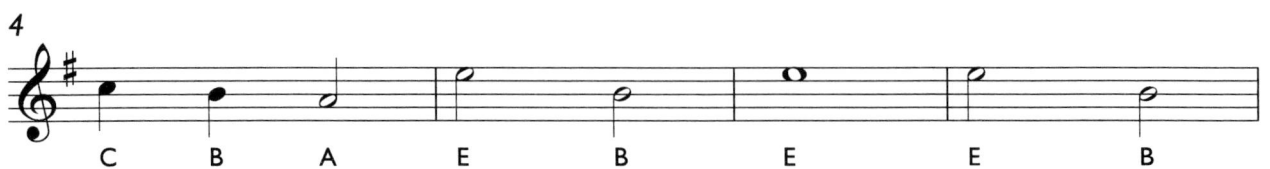
tuned percussion
(pre-level 1)

mp
E   B   G   E

E   B   G   C   E   B

A   E   B   B   G   G

Moderately 118

counter melody
(pre-level 1)

mp
E E E   E E E E   B

C B A   E   B   E   E   B

C B A   E   B   G

class music bumper pack
keyboard, counter melody and tuned percussion

1. Starting Out

keyboard
(pre-level 1)

Moderately 118

class music bumper pack
keyboard, counter melody and tuned percussion

2. Happy Times

tuned percussion
(pre-level 1)

Allegretto 120

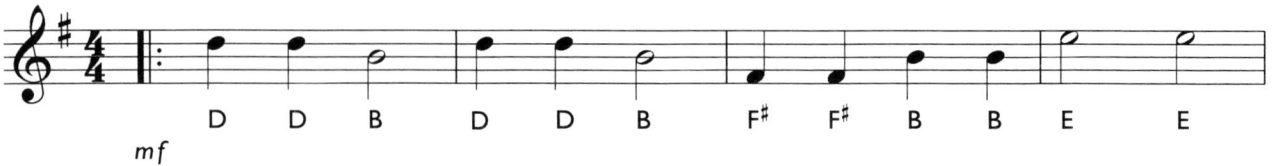

D D B D D B F# F# B B E E

5

D D B D D B F# F# B B G G

Allegretto 120

counter melody
(pre-level 1)

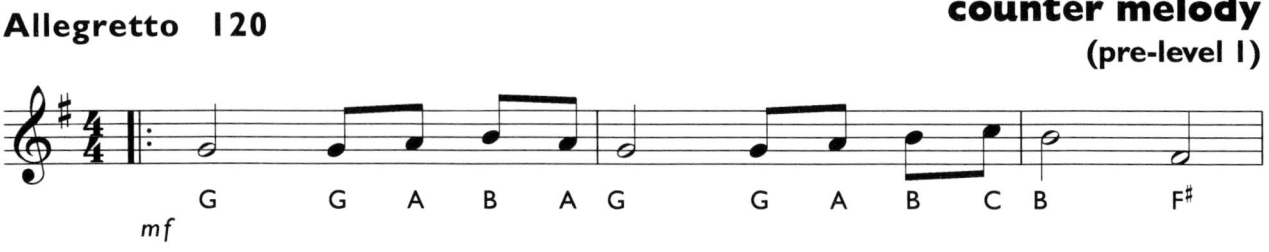

G G A B A G G A B C B F#

4

G E G G A B A G G A B C

7

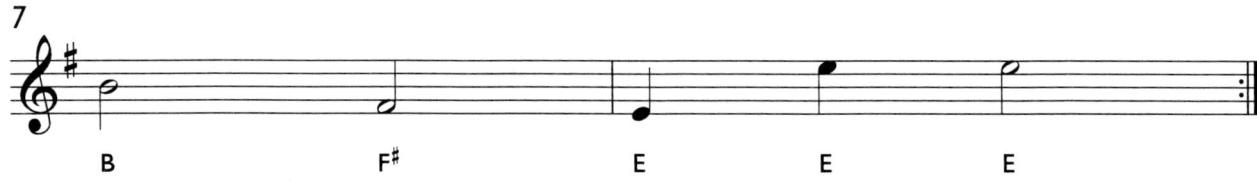

B F# E E E

class music bumper pack
keyboard, counter melody and tuned percussion

2. Happy Times

keyboard
(pre-level 1)

3. Spring

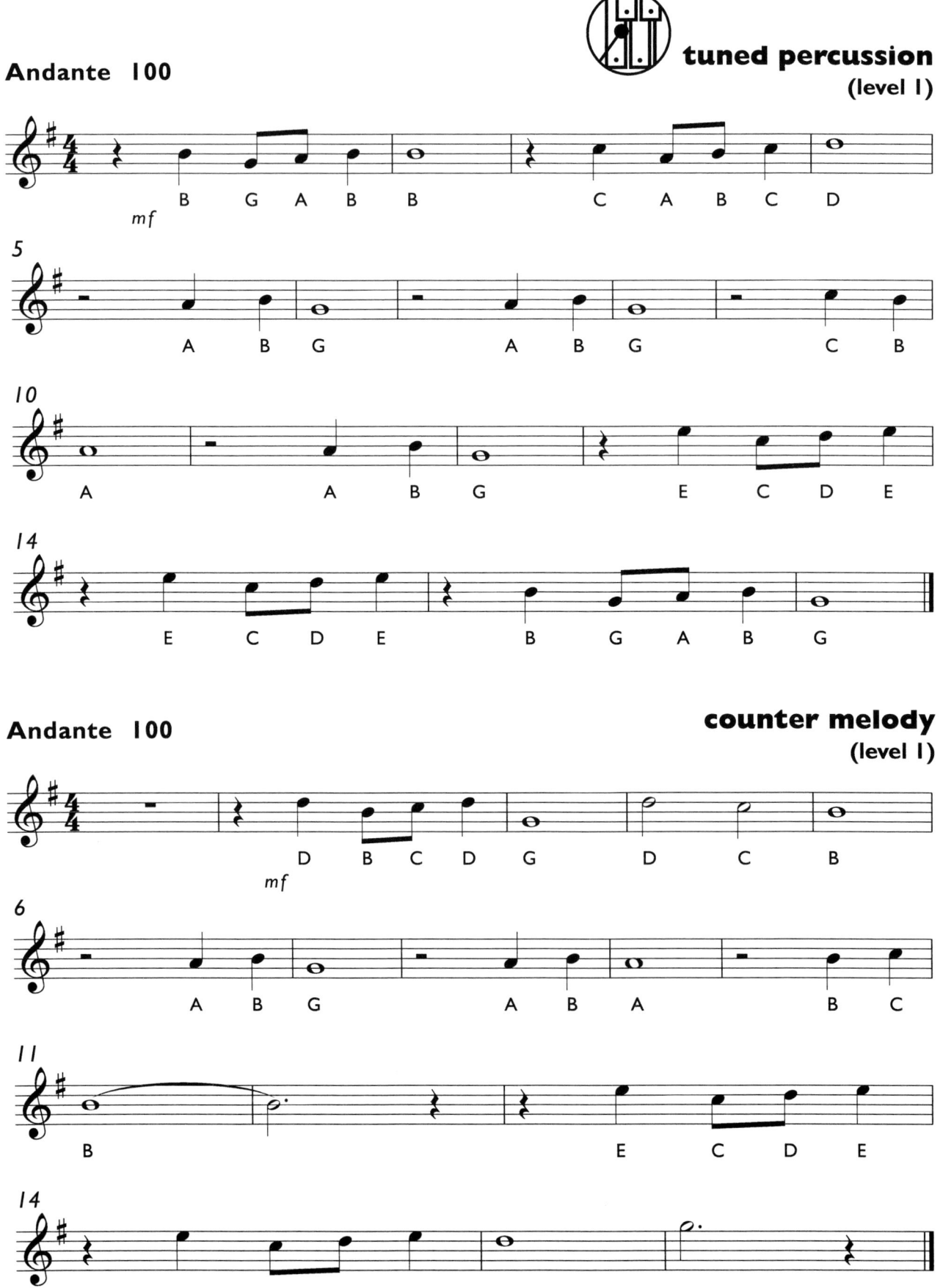

Andante 100

tuned percussion
(level 1)

Andante 100

counter melody
(level 1)

class music bumper pack
keyboard, counter melody and tuned percussion

3. Spring

keyboard
(pre-level 1)

Andante 100

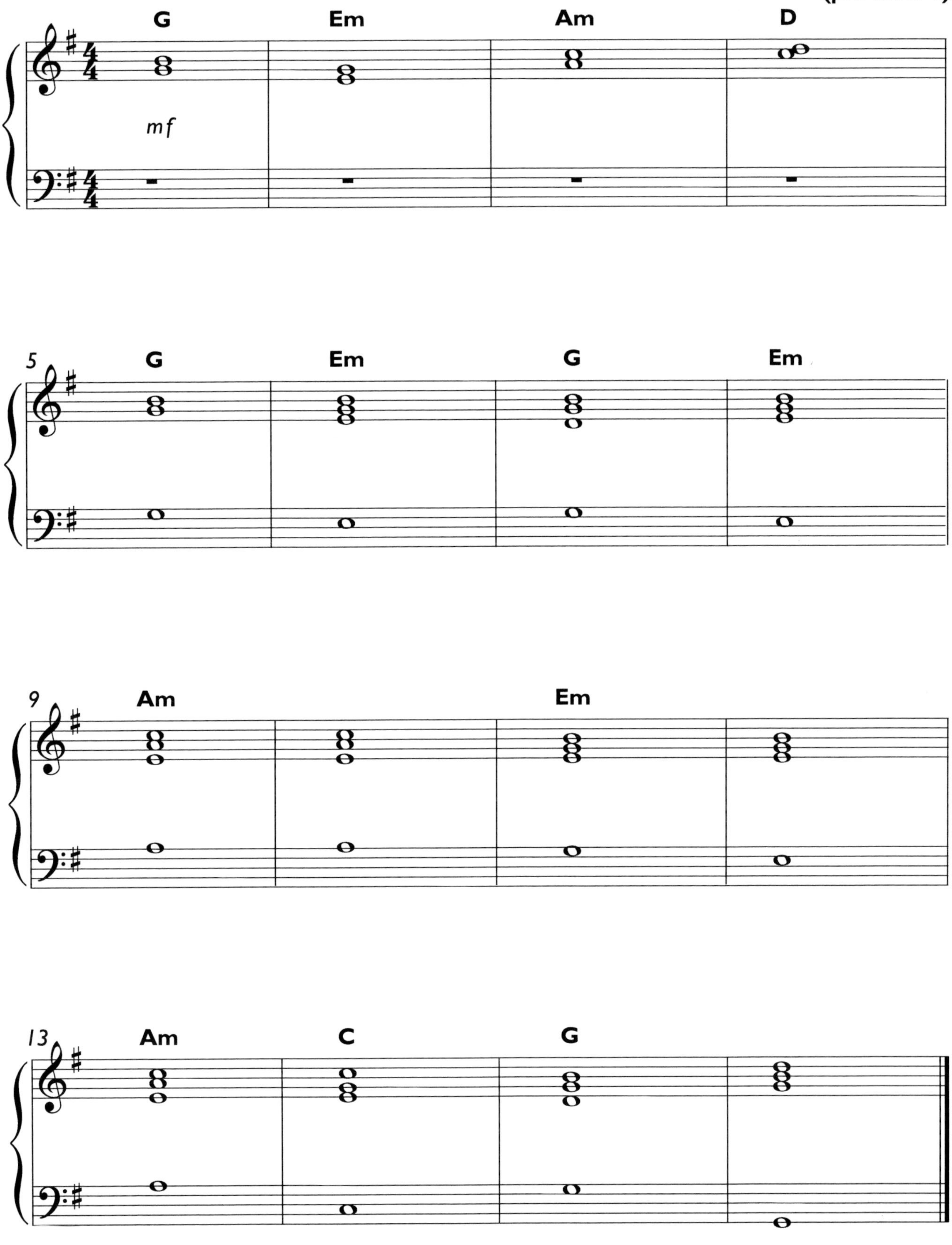

(Musical score: 16 bars in G major, 4/4 time, arranged in four systems of four bars each.)

System 1 (bars 1–4): **G** — **Em** — **Am** — **D**, marked *mf*

System 2 (bars 5–8): **G** — **Em** — **G** — **Em**

System 3 (bars 9–12): **Am** — (Am) — **Em** — (Em)

System 4 (bars 13–16): **Am** — **C** — **G** — (G)

class music bumper pack
keyboard, counter melody and tuned percussion

4. Italian Sunset

tuned percussion
(pre-level 1)

Adagio 90

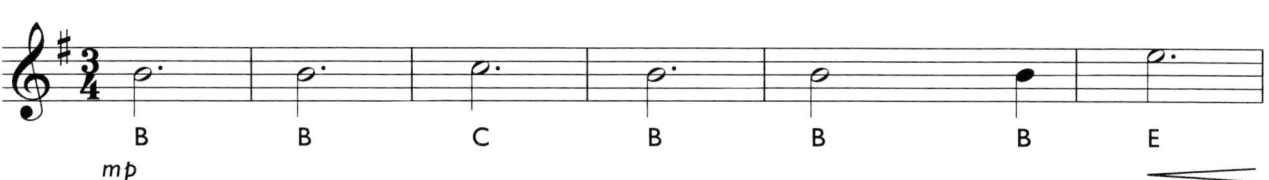

B   B   C   B   B   B   E
mp

7
F#   B   G   F#   E   G   F#   E
mf   *mp*

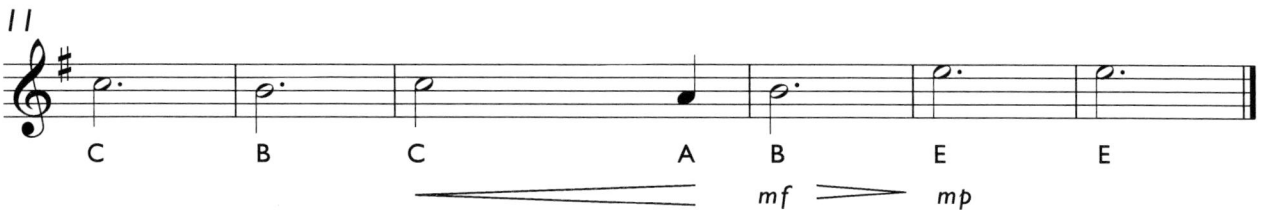

11
C   B   C   A   B   E   E
mf   *mp*

Adagio 90

counter melody
(level 1)

E   F#   G   G   A   B   C   D   B
mp

5
E   B   F#   B   F#   G   E   F#   G
mf   *mp*

10
G   A   B   C   D   B

13
E   B   E   B   E
mf   *mp*

class music bumper pack
keyboard, counter melody and tuned percussion

4. Italian Sunset

keyboard
(level 1)

Adagio 90

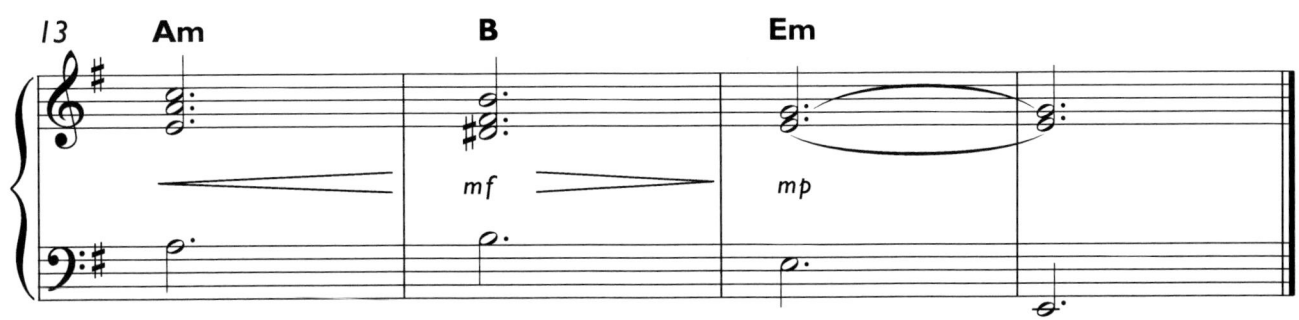

class music bumper pack
keyboard, counter melody and tuned percussion

5. One More Time

Andante 100

tuned percussion
(pre-level 1)

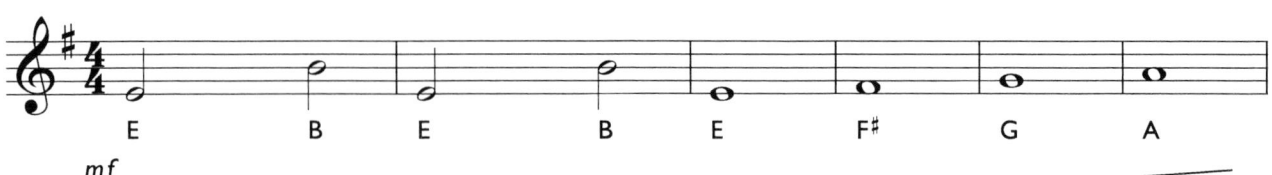

E B E B E F# G A

mf

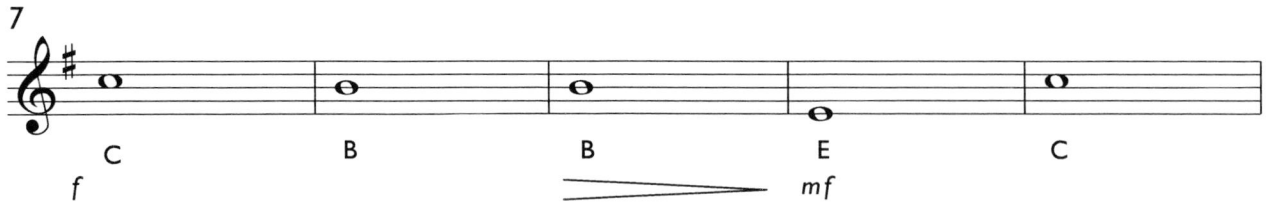

7

C B B E C

f *mf*

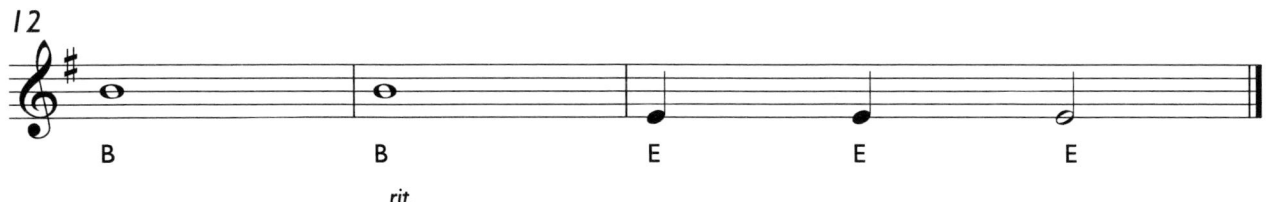

12

B B E E E

rit.

Andante 100

counter melody
(pre-level 1)

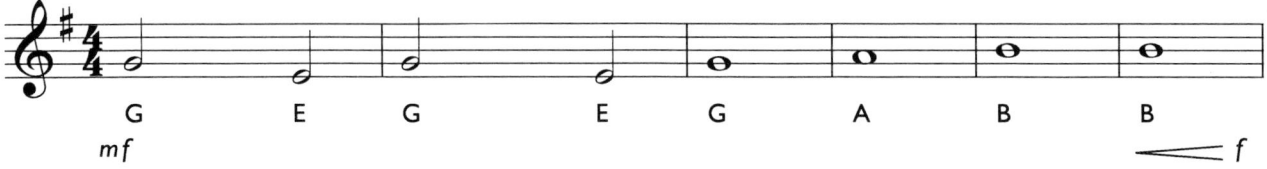

G E G E G A B B

mf *f*

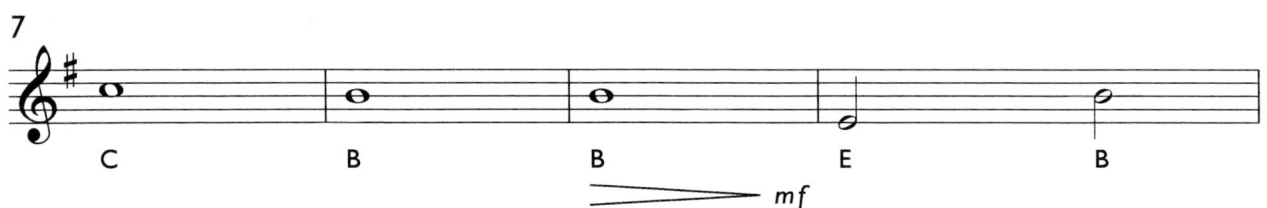

7

C B B E B

mf

11

C B B E

rit.

class music bumper pack
keyboard, counter melody and tuned percussion

5. One More Time

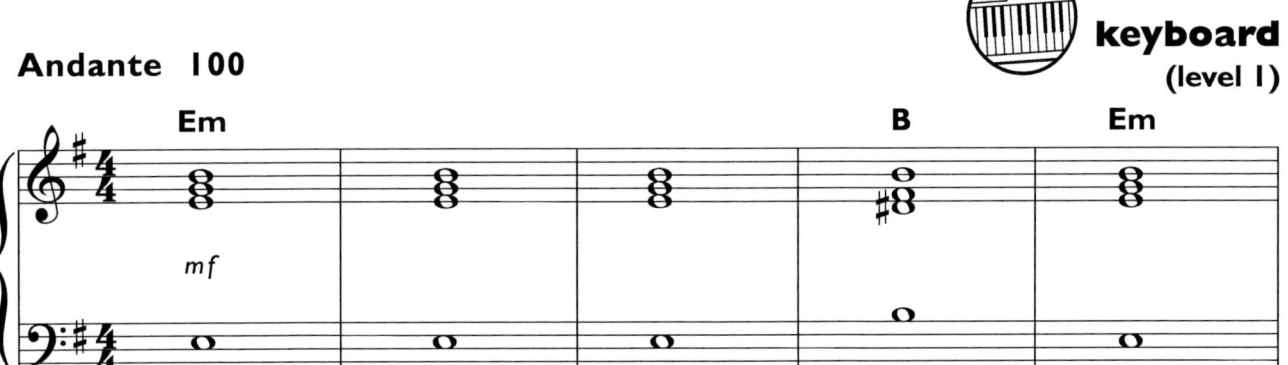

Andante 100

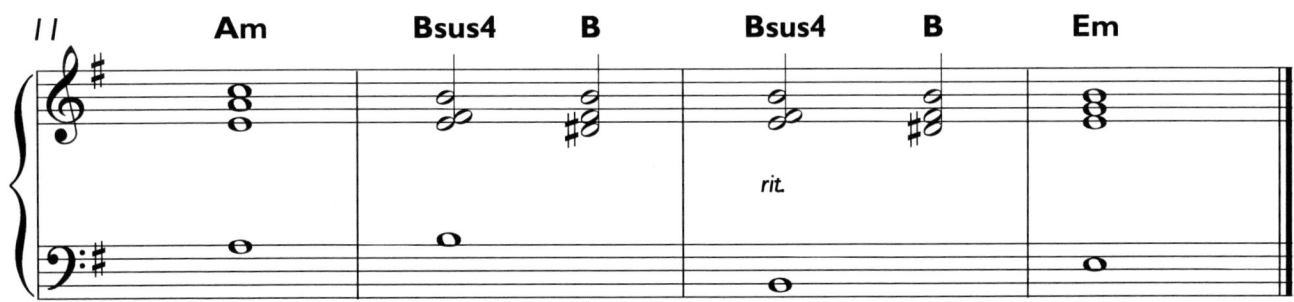

class music bumper pack
keyboard, counter melody and tuned percussion

19

6. Lazy Waltz

Andante 100

tuned percussion
(level 1)

counter melody
(pre-level 1)

Andante 100

class music bumper pack
keyboard, counter melody and tuned percussion

6. Lazy Waltz

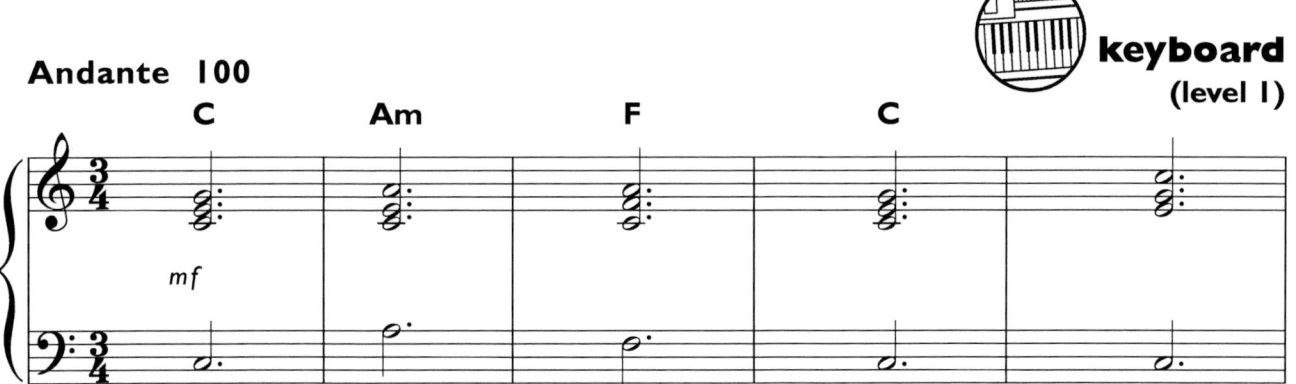

keyboard
(level 1)

Andante 100

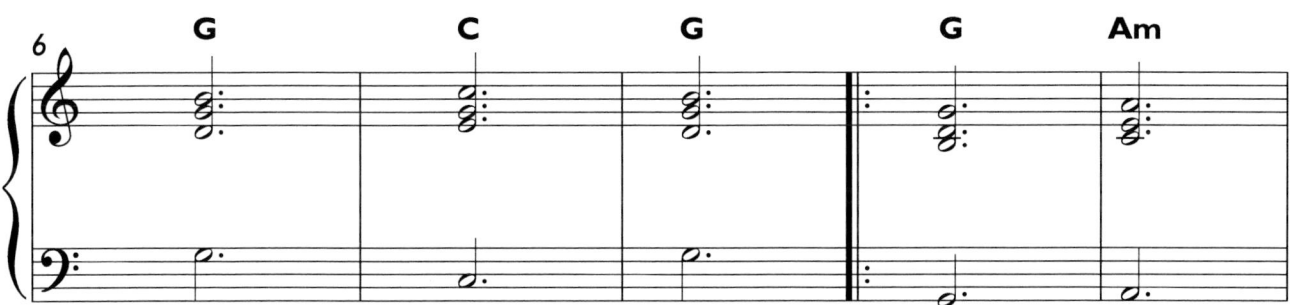

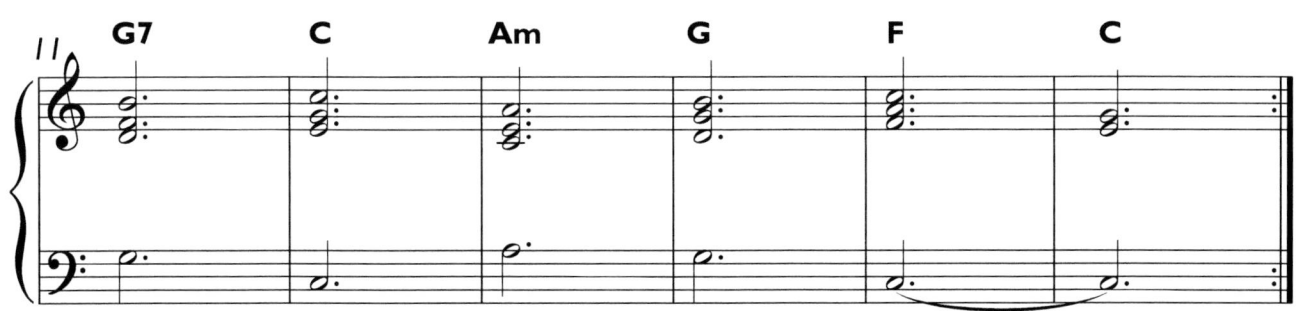

class music bumper pack
keyboard, counter melody and tuned percussion

21

7. Far and Away

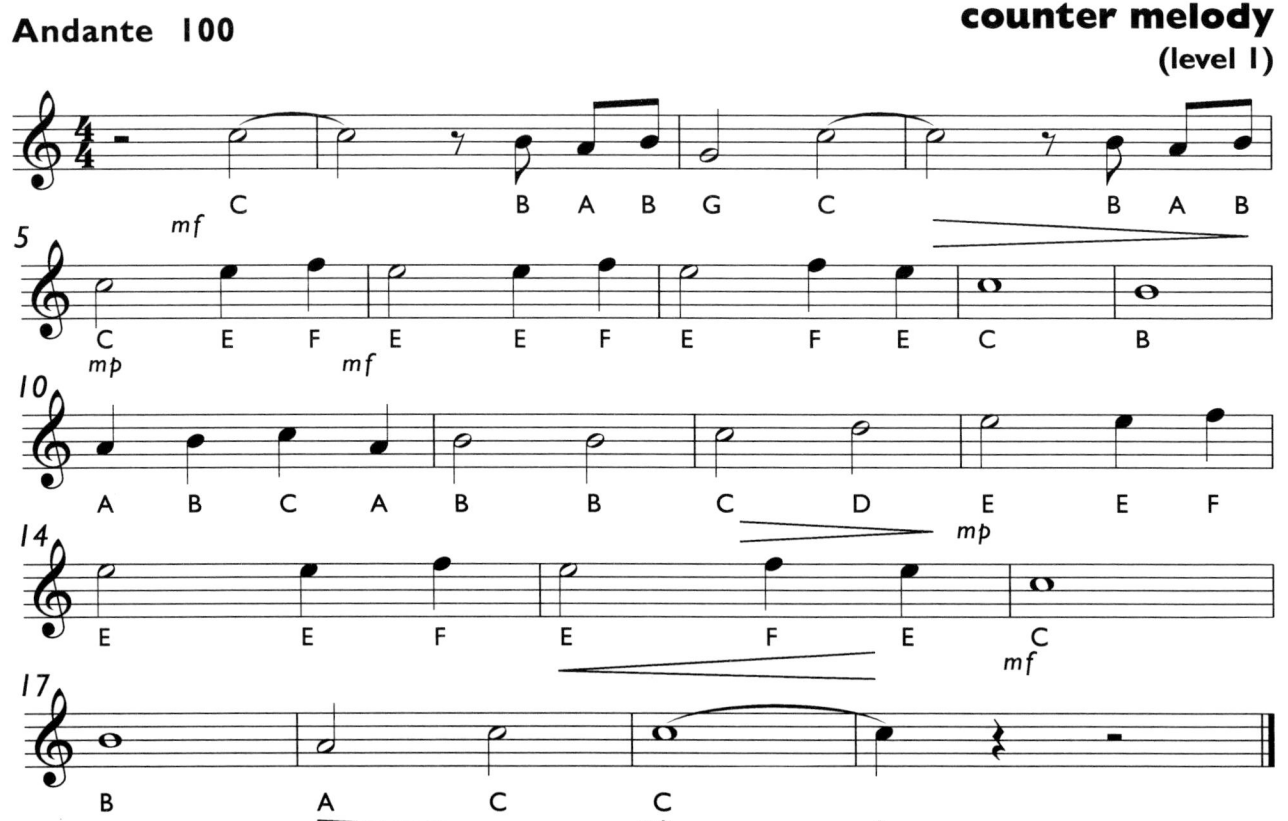

class music bumper pack
keyboard, counter melody and tuned percussion

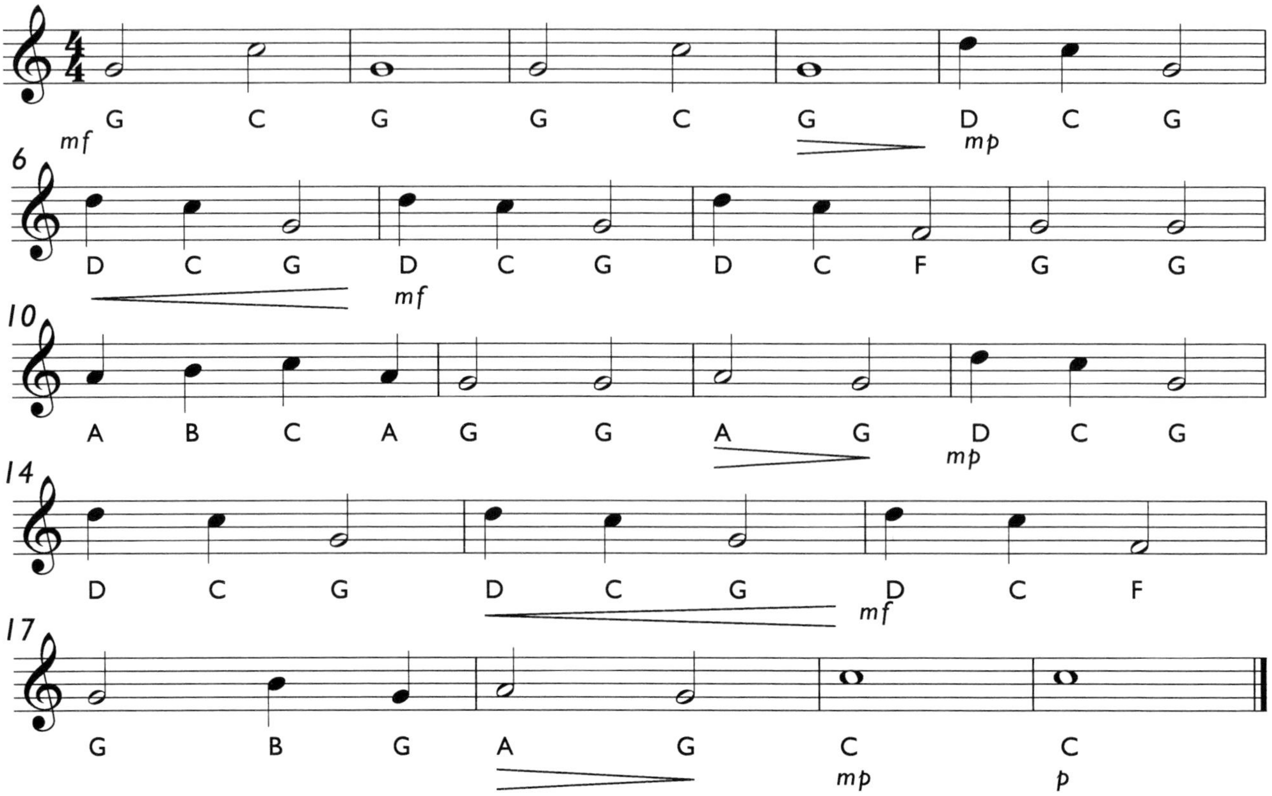

© Leckie & Leckie

7. Far and Away

keyboard
(level 1)

8. Sushi

tuned percussion
(level 1)

Andante 95

counter melody
(level 1)

Andante 95

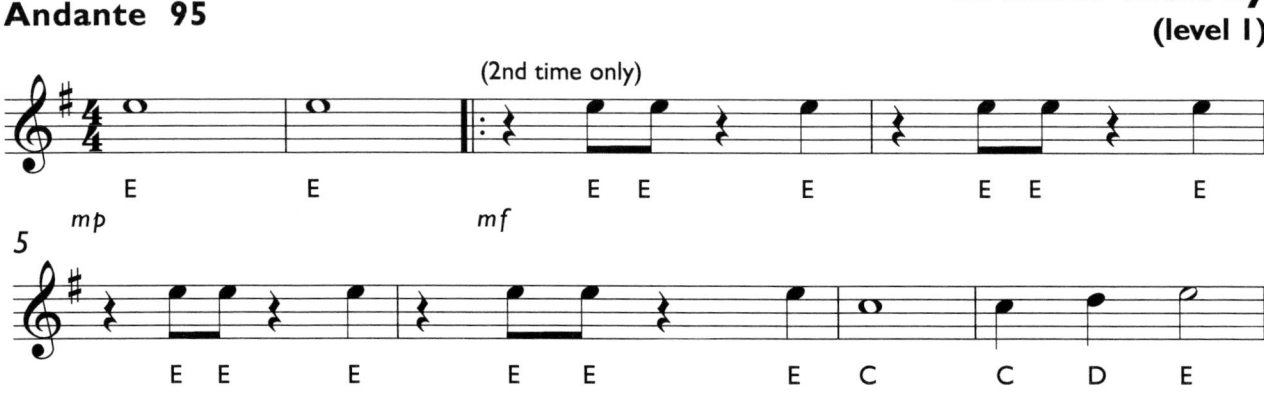

class music bumper pack
keyboard, counter melody and tuned percussion

8. Sushi

keyboard
(level 2)

Andante 95

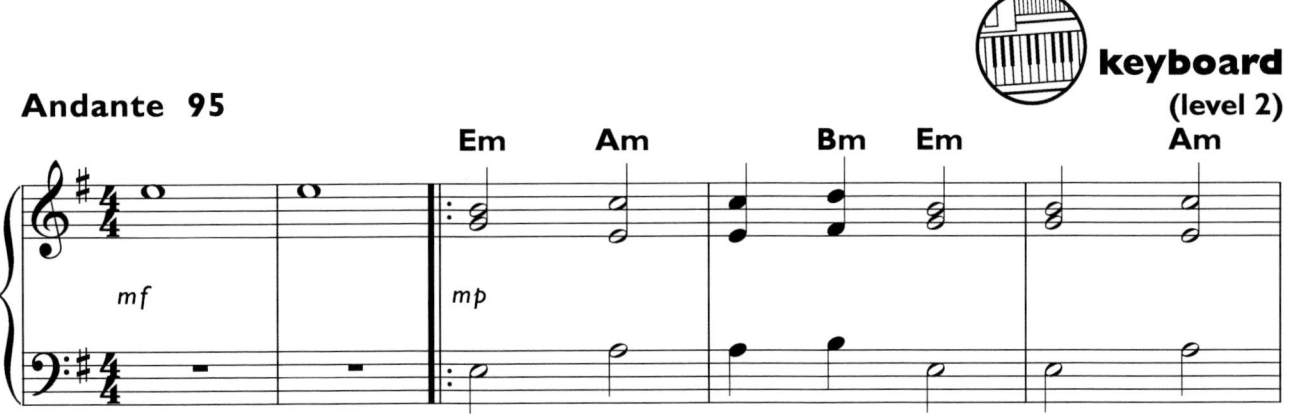

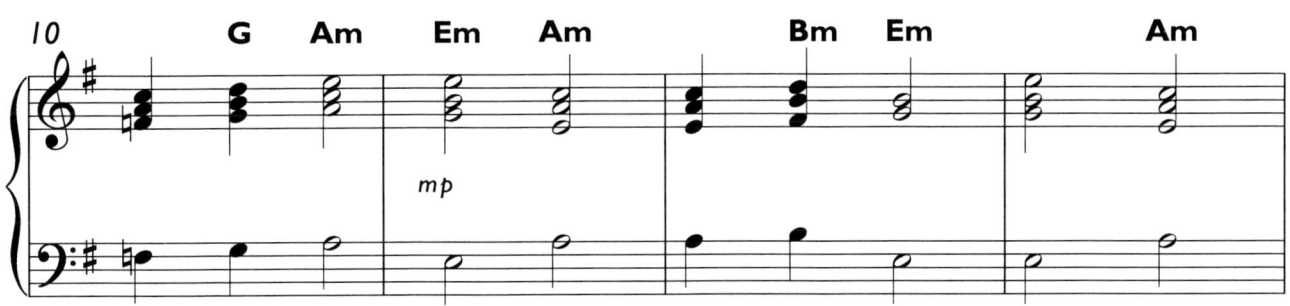

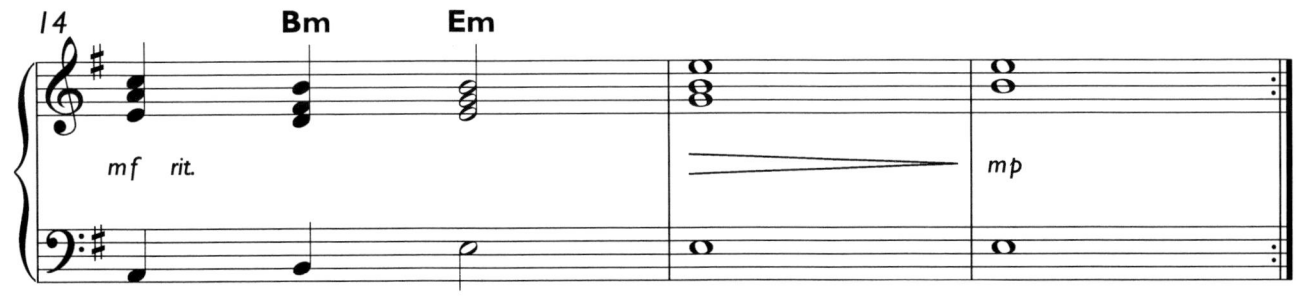

9. Wash and Go

Allegretto 112

tuned percussion
(level 2)

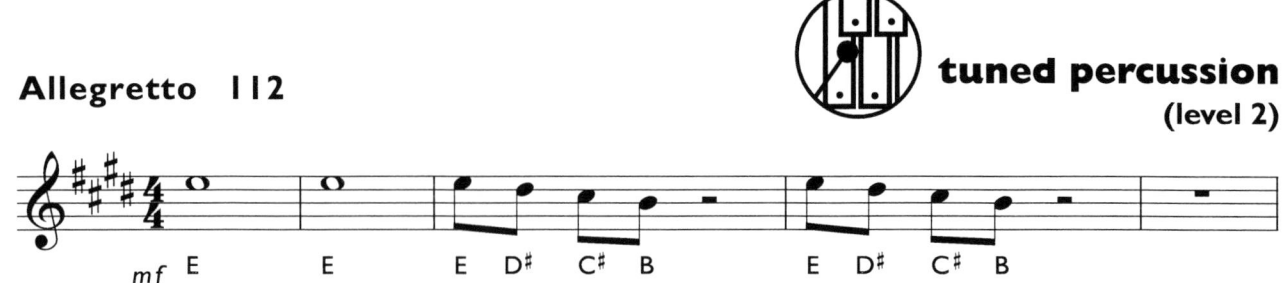

mf E   E   E D# C# B   E D# C# B

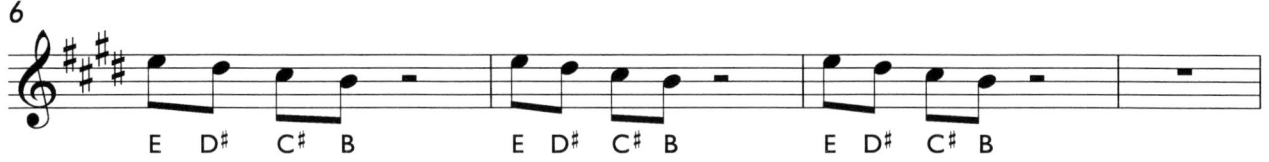

6

E D# C# B   E D# C# B   E D# C# B

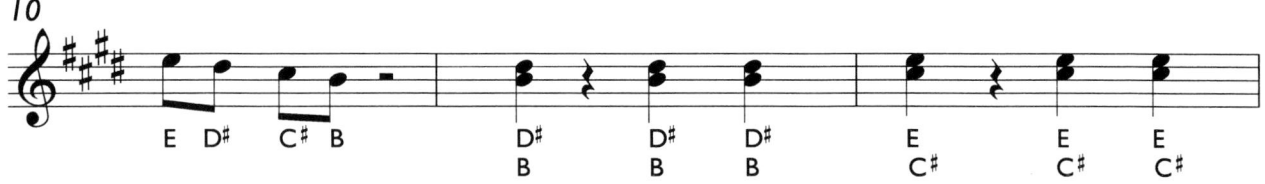

10

E D# C# B   D#   D#   D#   E   E   E
             B   B   B   C#   C#   C#

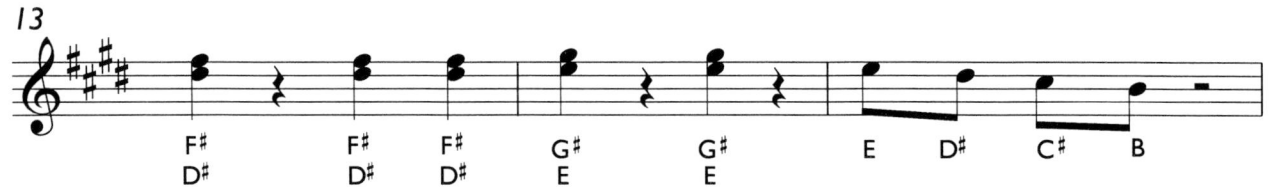

13

F#   F#   F#   G#   G#   E D# C# B
D#   D#   D#   E   E

16

E D# C# B   B   F#   E

9. Wash and Go

counter melody
(level 1)

Allegretto 112

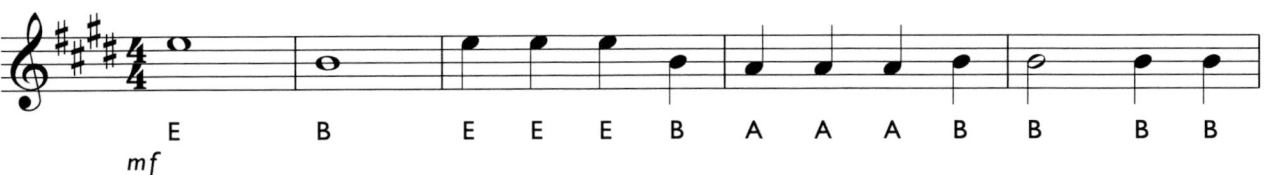

E B E E E B A A A B B B B

mf

6

E E E E B B A A A F# F# F# E

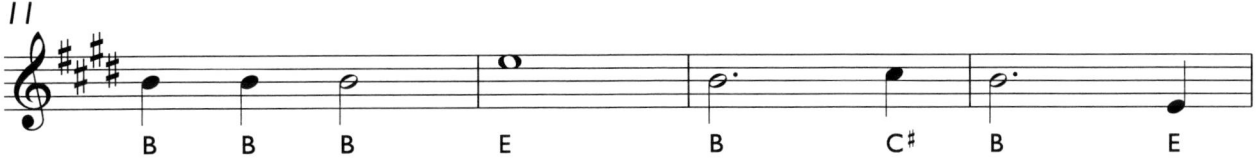

11

B B B E B C# B E

15

B E B A B F# E

9. Wash and Go

Allegretto 112

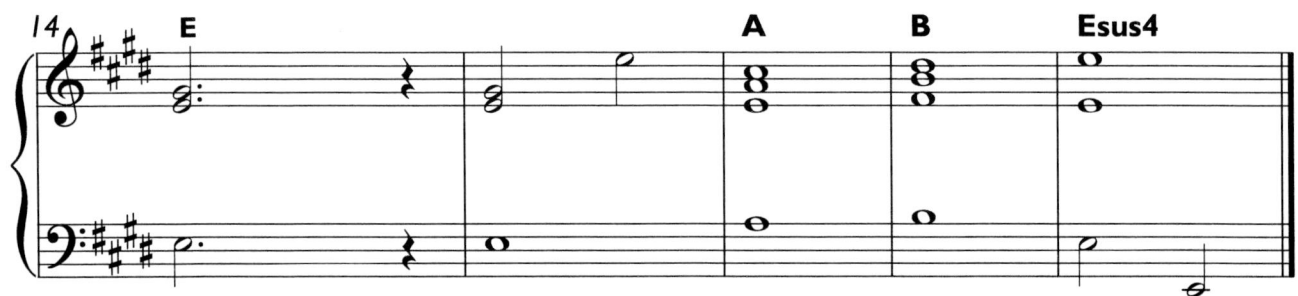

class music bumper pack
keyboard, counter melody and tuned percussion

10. A French Affair

tuned percussion
(level 1)

counter melody
(level 1)

class music bumper pack
keyboard, counter melody and tuned percussion

29

10. A French Affair

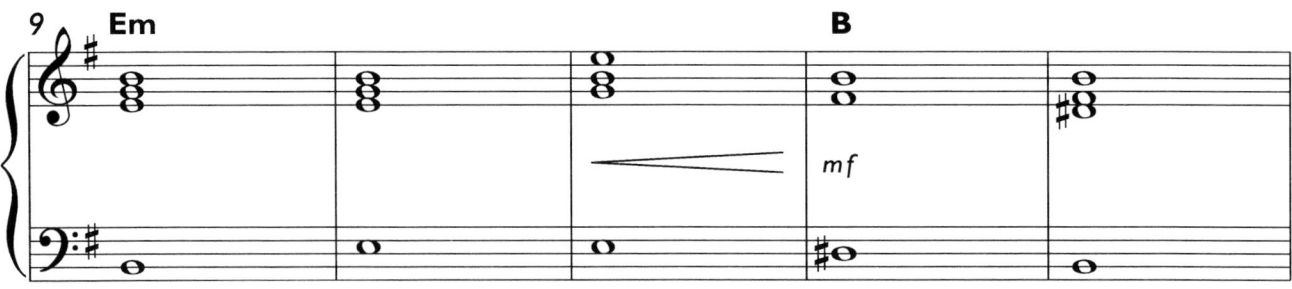

keyboard
(level 2)

Adagio 82

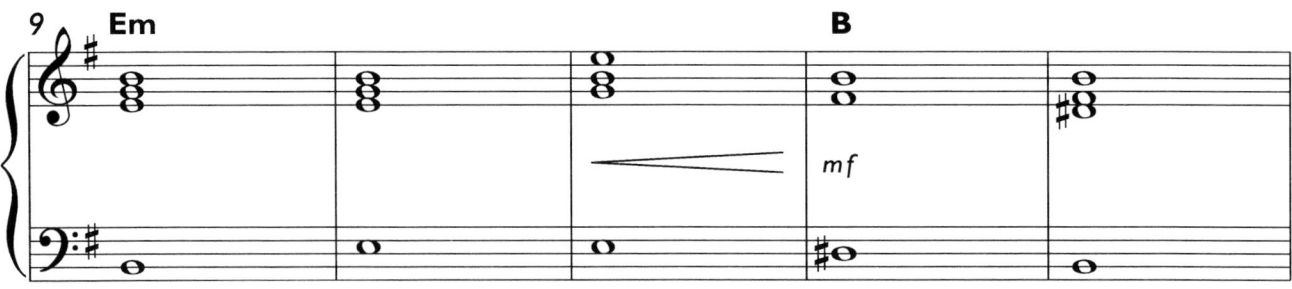

class music bumper pack
keyboard, counter melody and tuned percussion

11. Everythin's OK

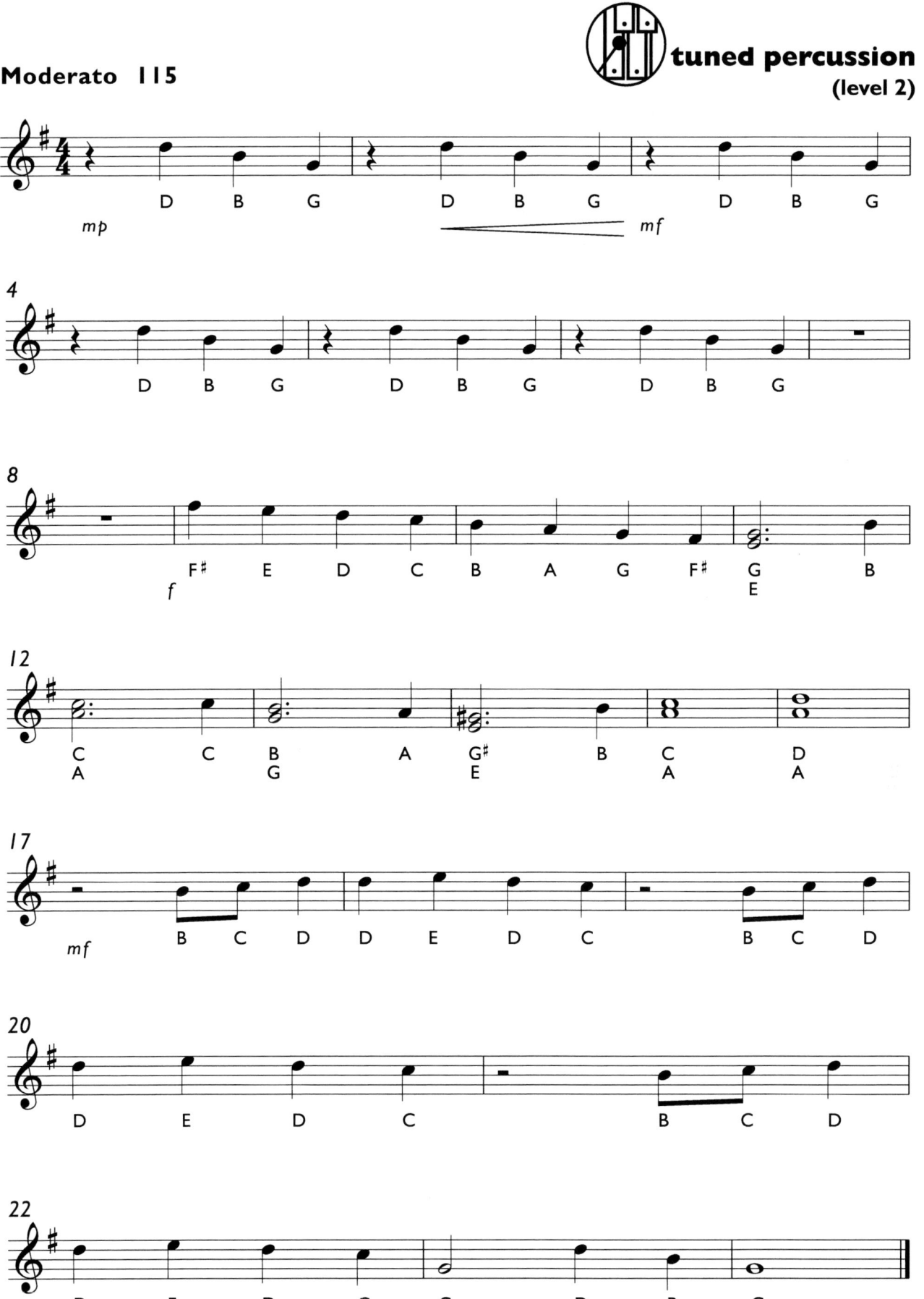

tuned percussion
(level 2)

Moderato 115

11. Everythin's OK

counter melody
(level 1)

Moderato 115

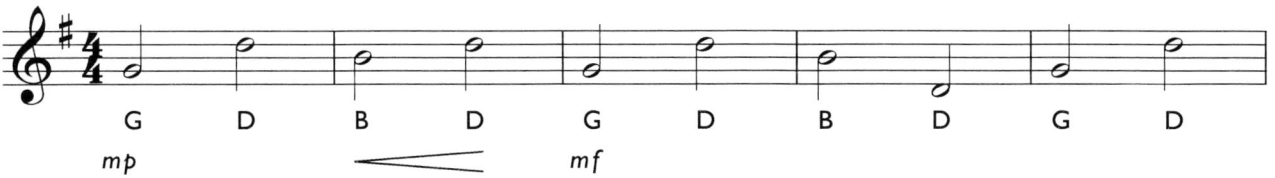

G   D   B   D   G   D   B   D   G   D

mp   mf

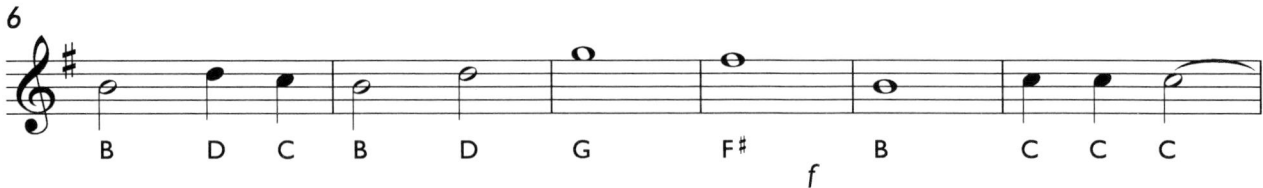

B   D   C   B   D   G   F#   B   C   C   C

f

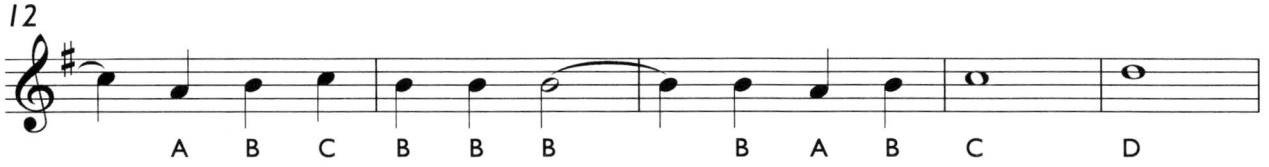

A   B   C   B   B   B   B   A   B   C   D

B   C   D   D   D   B   C   D   D   D

mf

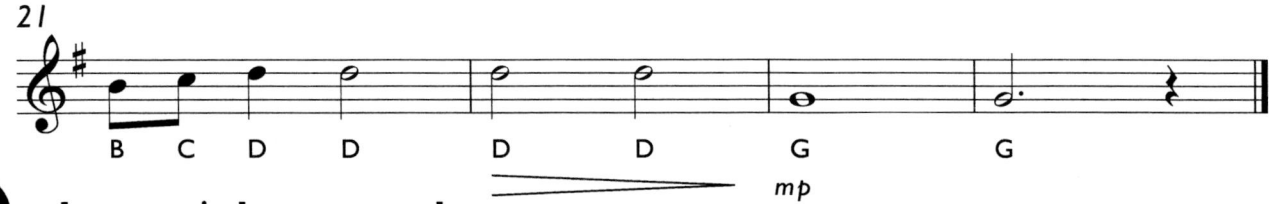

B   C   D   D   D   D   G   G

mp

32

class music bumper pack
keyboard, counter melody and tuned percussion

© Leckie & Leckie

11. Everythin's OK

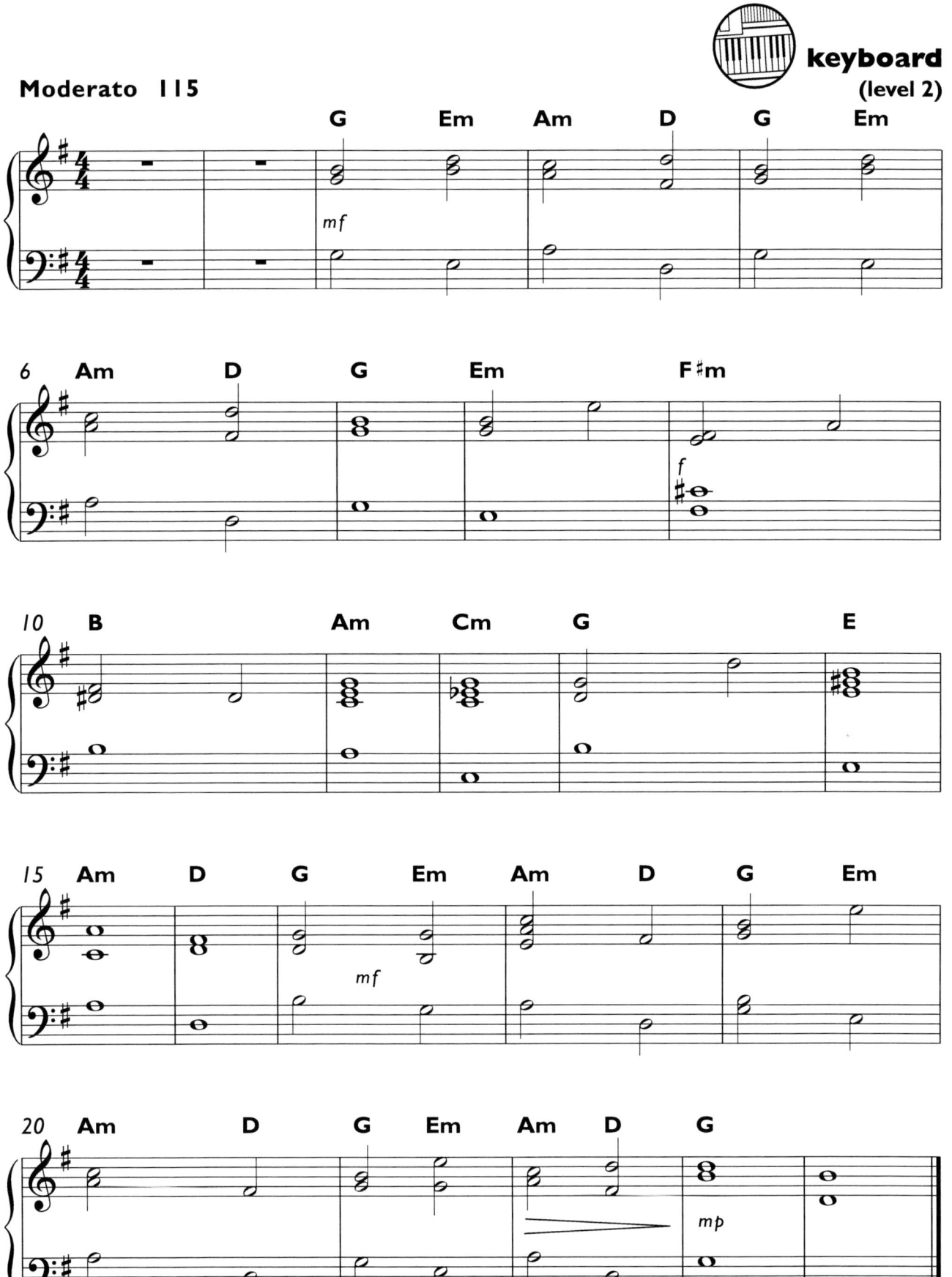

Moderato 115

12. One of These Days

tuned percussion
(level 2)

Allegro 120

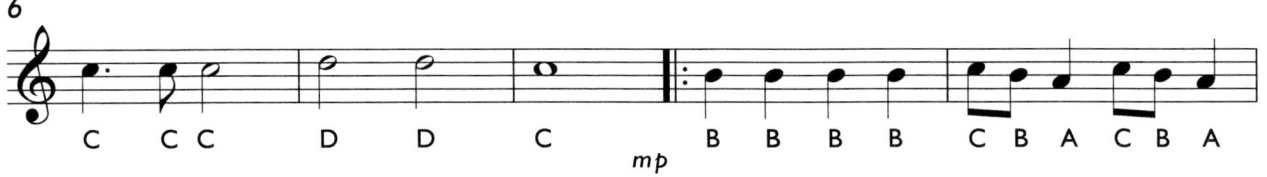

counter melody
(level 1)

Allegro 120

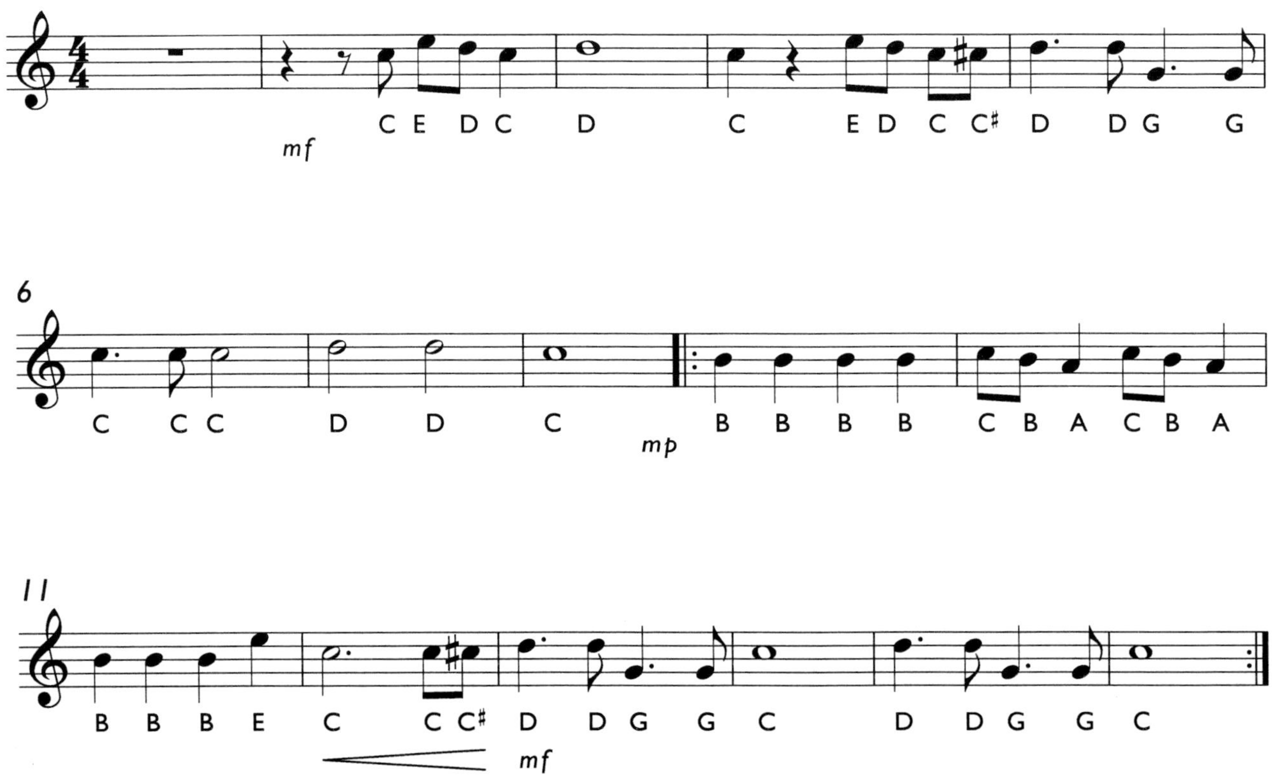

class music bumper pack
keyboard, counter melody and tuned percussion

© Leckie & Leckie

12. One of These Days

keyboard
(level 2)

Allegro 120

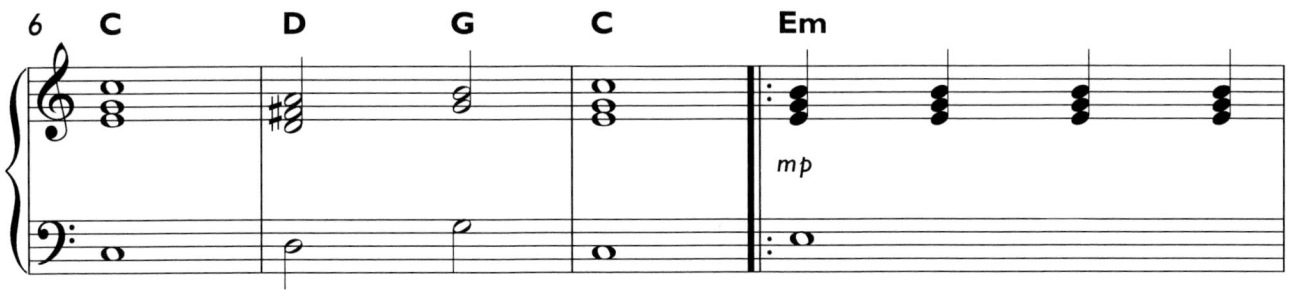

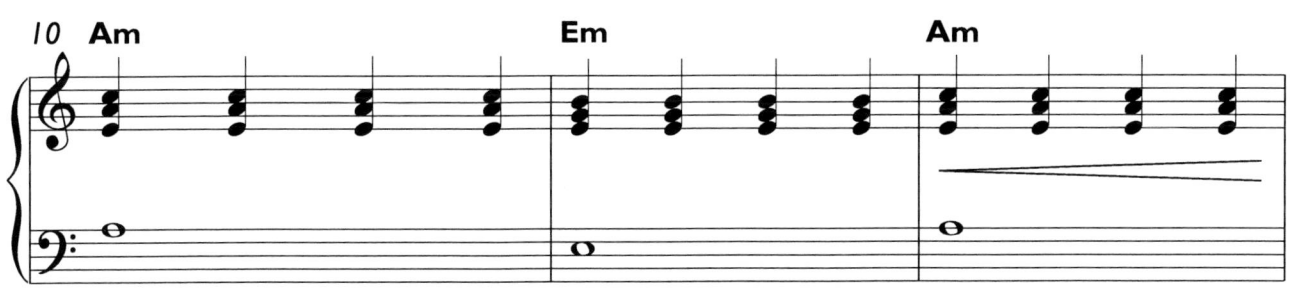

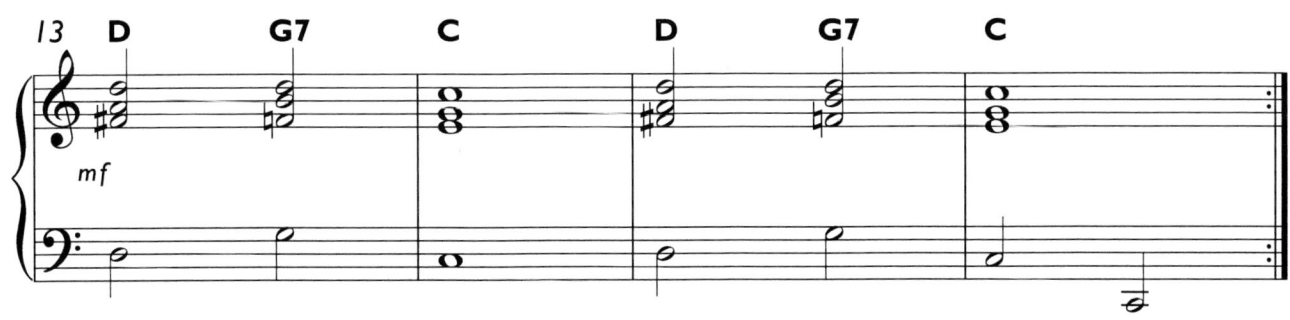

13. Told You So

tuned percussion
(level 2)

Andante 100

counter melody
(level 1)

Andante 100

class music bumper pack
keyboard, counter melody and tuned percussion

© Leckie & Leckie

13. Told You So

keyboard
(level 2)

Andante 100

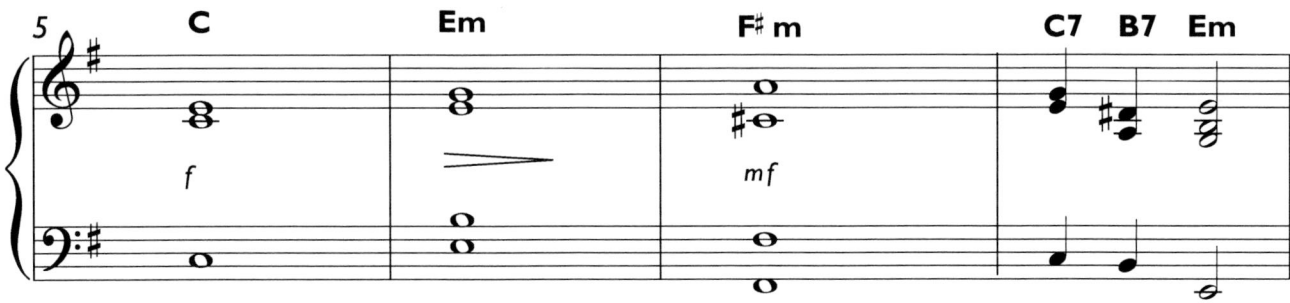

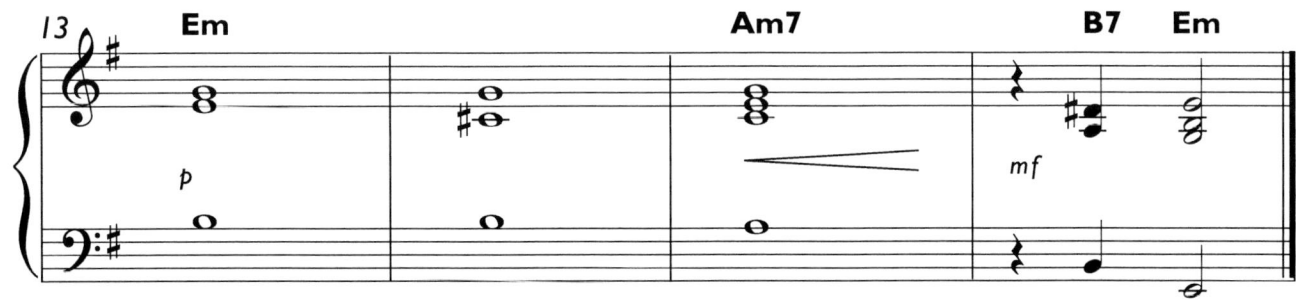

keyboard, counter melody and tuned percussion

14. Silver Swan

Moderate Soul 100

Moderate Soul 100

14. Silver Swan

keyboard
(level 1)

Moderate Soul 100

15. Comin' Home

tuned percussion
(level 2)

Andante 100

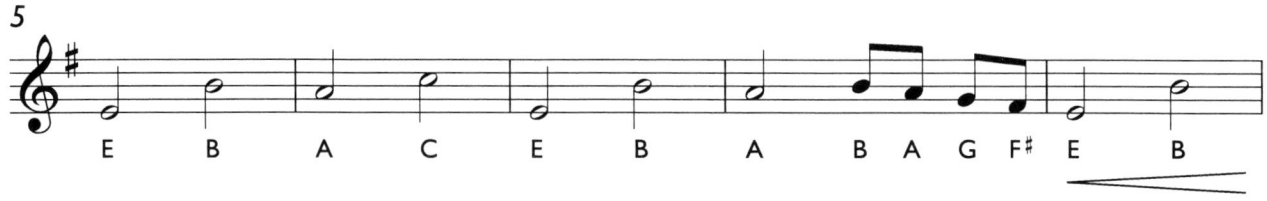

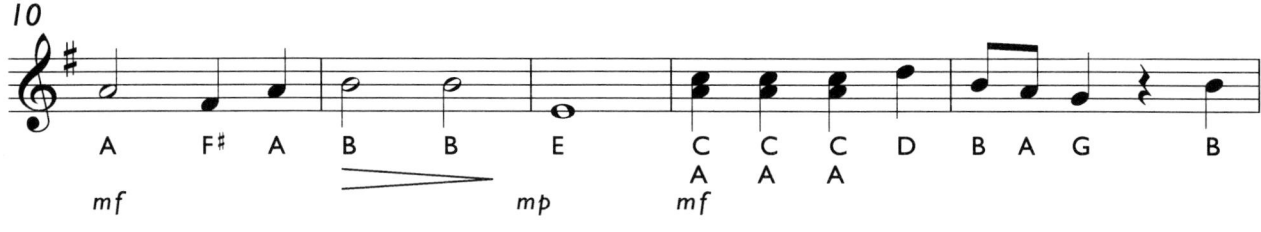

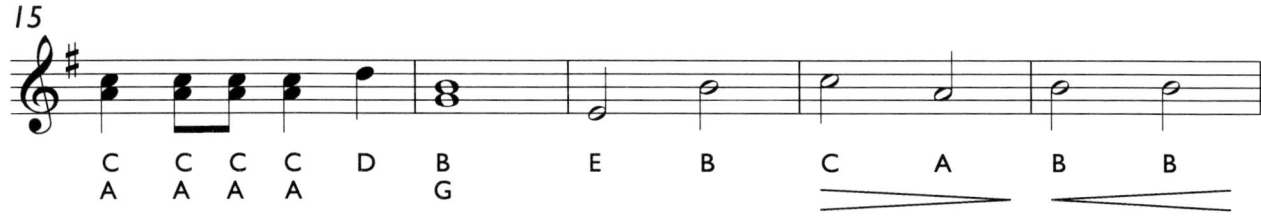

class music bumper pack
keyboard, counter melody and tuned percussion

15. Comin' Home

counter melody
(level 2)

Andante 100

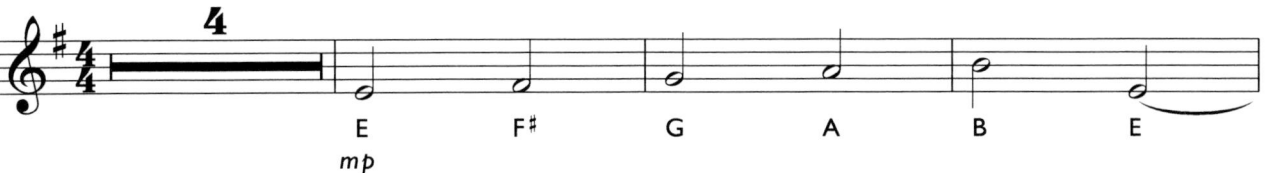

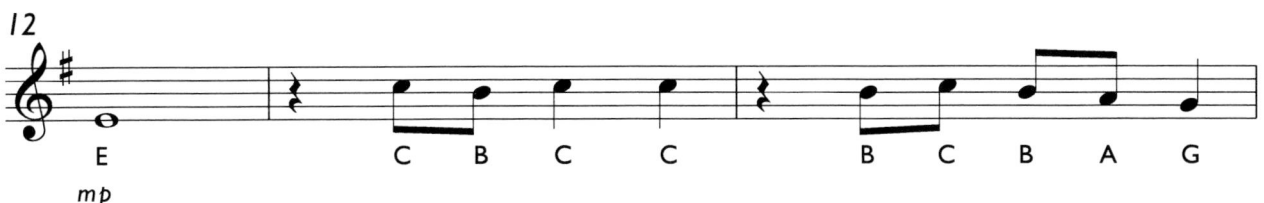

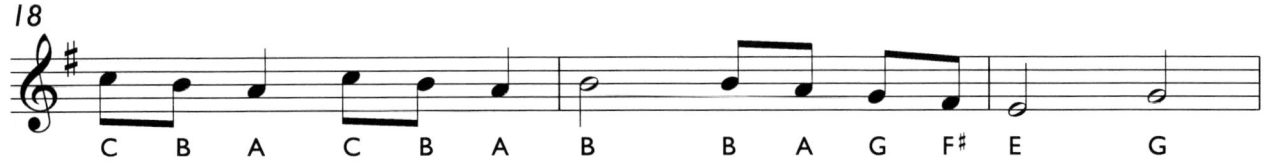

class music bumper pack
keyboard, counter melody and tuned percussion

15. Comin' Home

keyboard
(level 2)

Andante 100

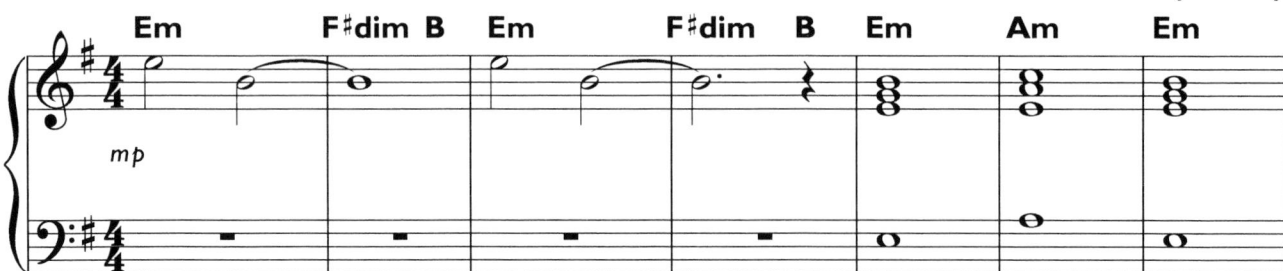

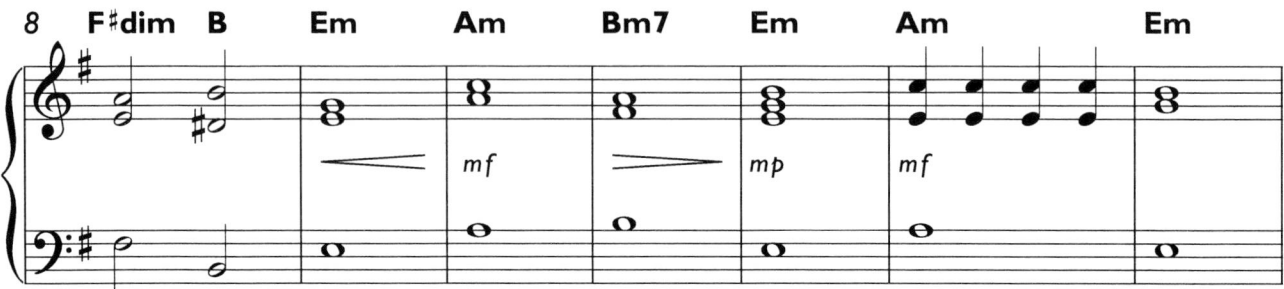

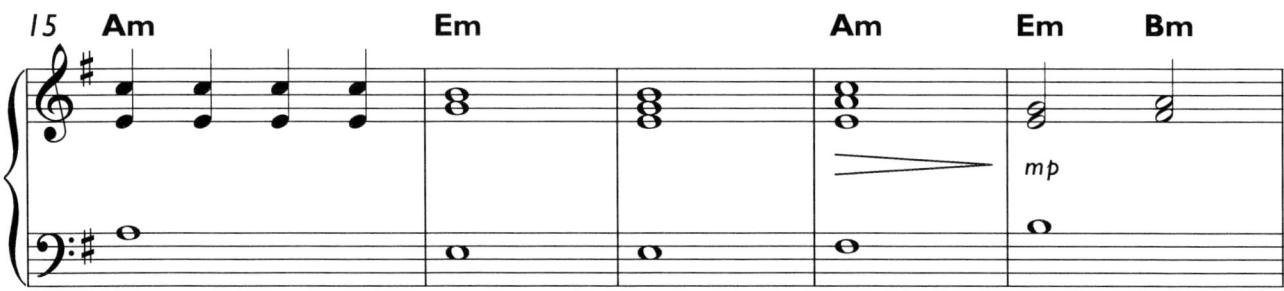

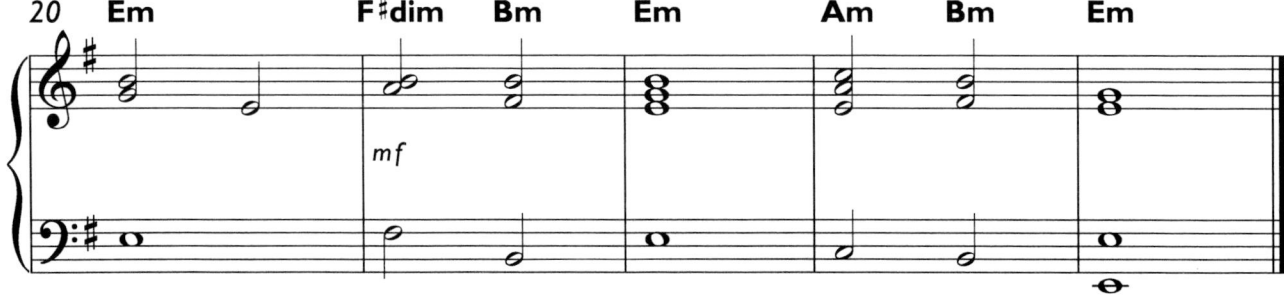

class music bumper pack
keyboard, counter melody and tuned percussion

16. Circle of Love

With Life 124

16. Circle of Love

With Life 124

4

f   E D   C D   G   D C   B C   G   E D   C D   G

8

A   C B   E D   C D   G   D C   B C   G   E D   C D   G

12

G   B C   *mf*   G   G   G   G F   E   E   E D   E F   G   G   G   G F

16

E   D   *f*   E D   C D   G   D C   B C   G   E D   C D   G

20

G   B C   D   G C   D   G A   F   E

class music bumper pack
keyboard, counter melody and tuned percussion

16. Circle of Love

keyboard
(level 2)

With Life 124

class music bumper pack
keyboard, counter melody and tuned percussion

17. Over and Over

Rock Feel III

tuned percussion
(level 2)

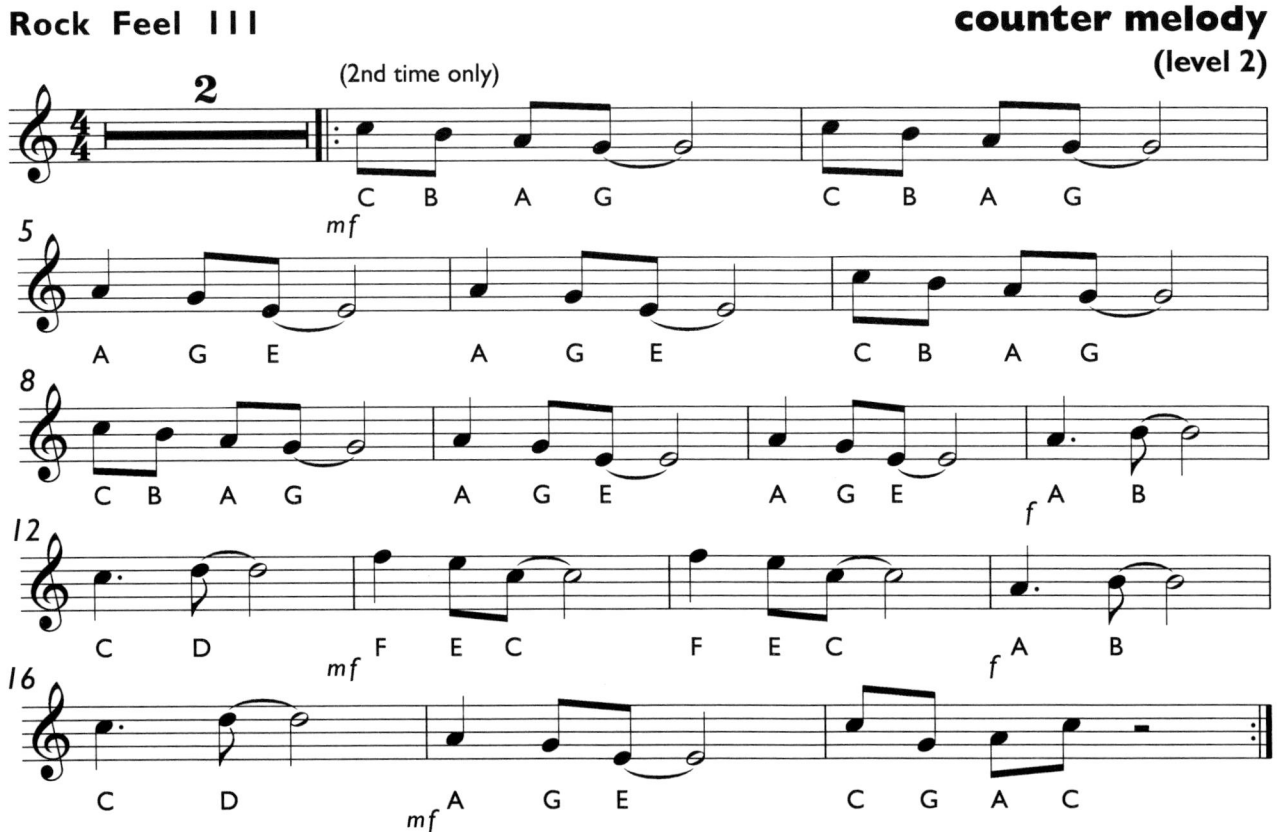

Rock Feel III

counter melody
(level 2)

class music bumper pack
keyboard, counter melody and tuned percussion

17. Over and Over

keyboard
(level 2)

Rock Feel ♩♩♩

keyboard, counter melody and tuned percussion

18. 2 Fret Waltz

Moderately 108

tuned percussion
(level 2)

18. 2 Fret Waltz

counter melody
(level 2)

Moderately 108

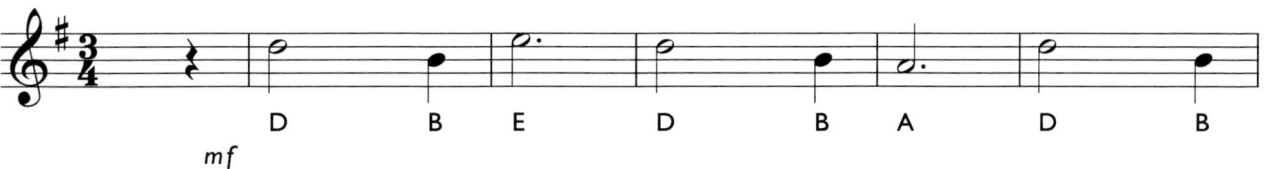

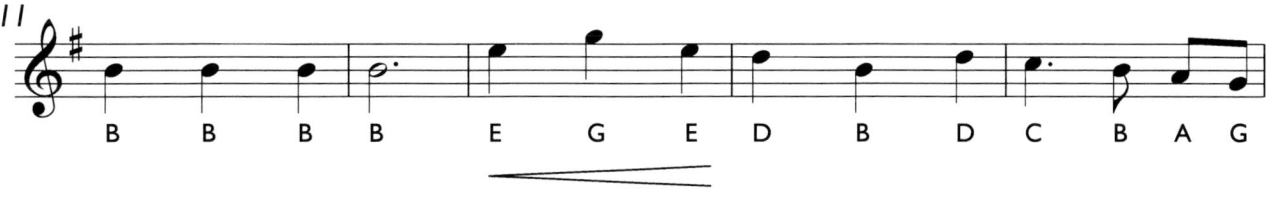

class music bumper pack
49
keyboard, counter melody and tuned percussion

18. 2 Fret Waltz

keyboard
(level 2)

Moderately 108

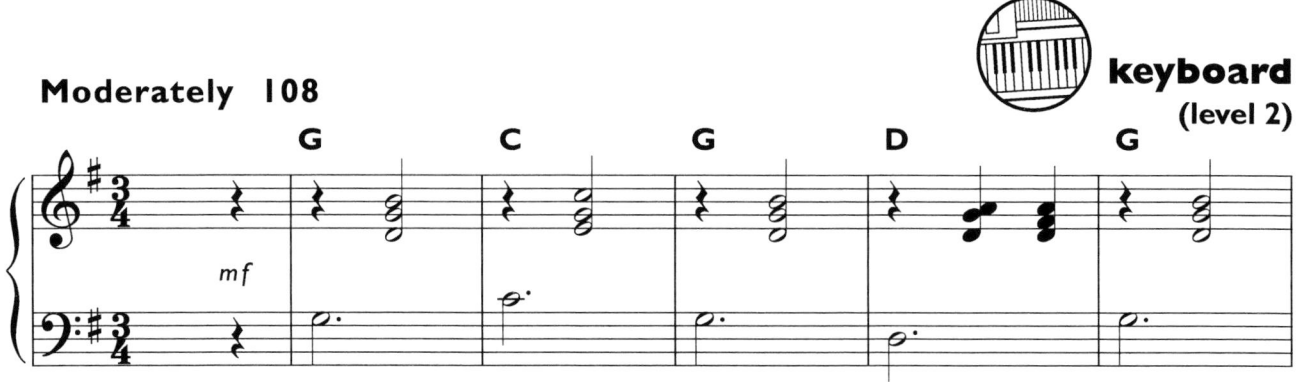

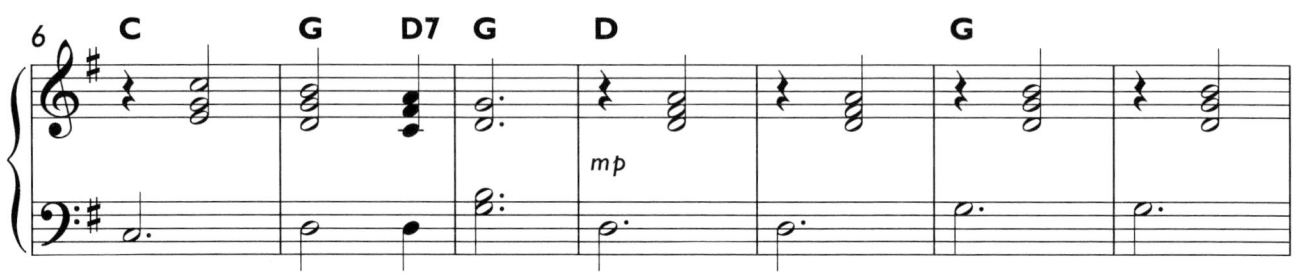

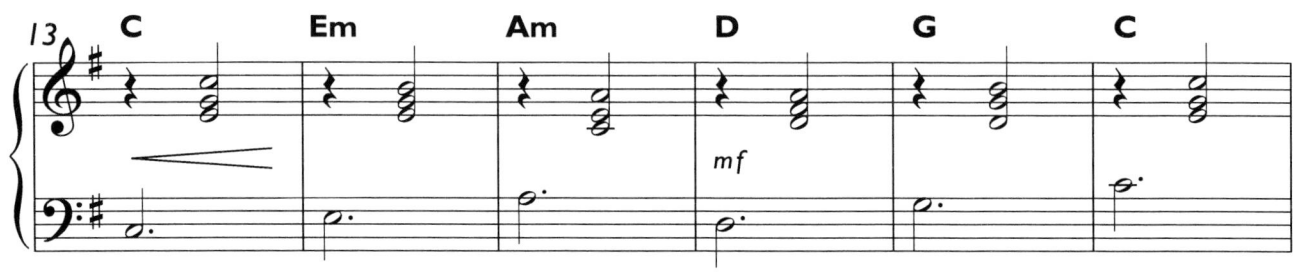

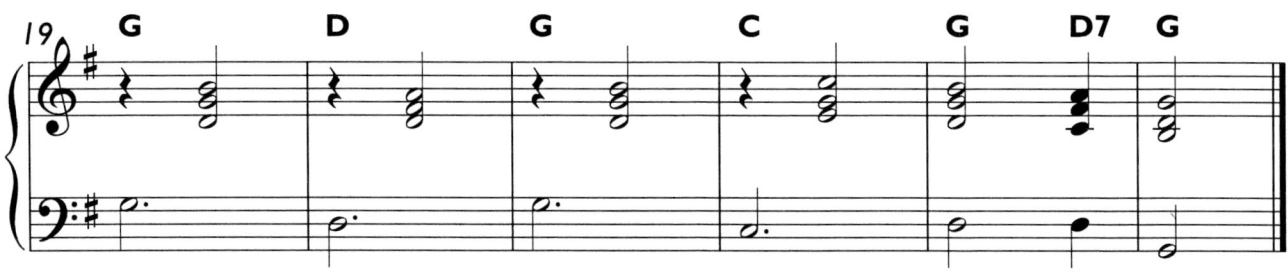

class music bumper pack
keyboard, counter melody and tuned percussion

19. Rumba

Latin Feel 120

tuned percussion
(level 2)

class music bumper pack
keyboard, counter melody and tuned percussion

19. Rumba

Latin Feel 120

f
E D E   C G G

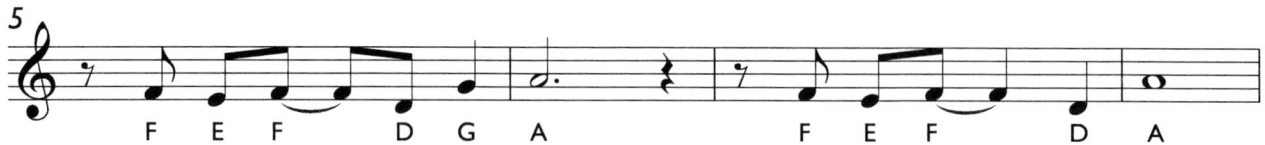

F E F   D G A   F E F   D A

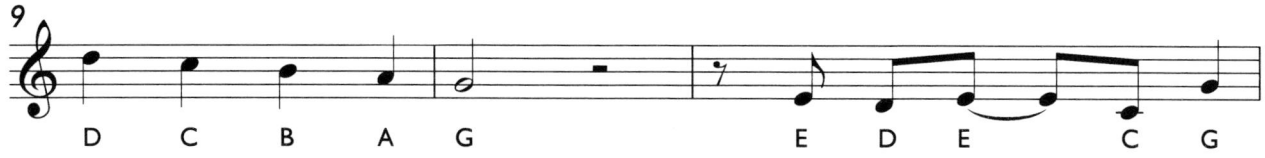

D C B A G   E D E   C G

G   A   B♭ A   F   E   D

E D E   C A G   G G G G C   C

class music bumper pack
keyboard, counter melody and tuned percussion

© Leckie & Leckie

19. Rumba

keyboard
(level 2)

Latin Feel 120

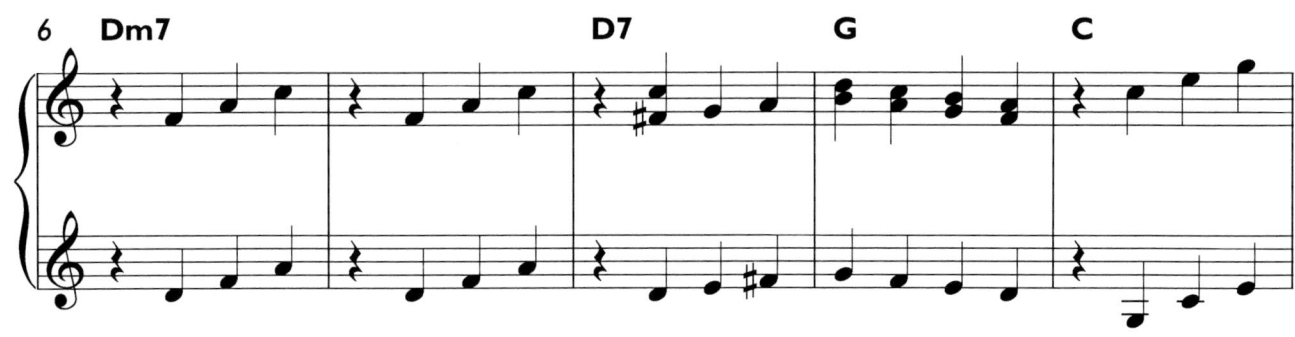

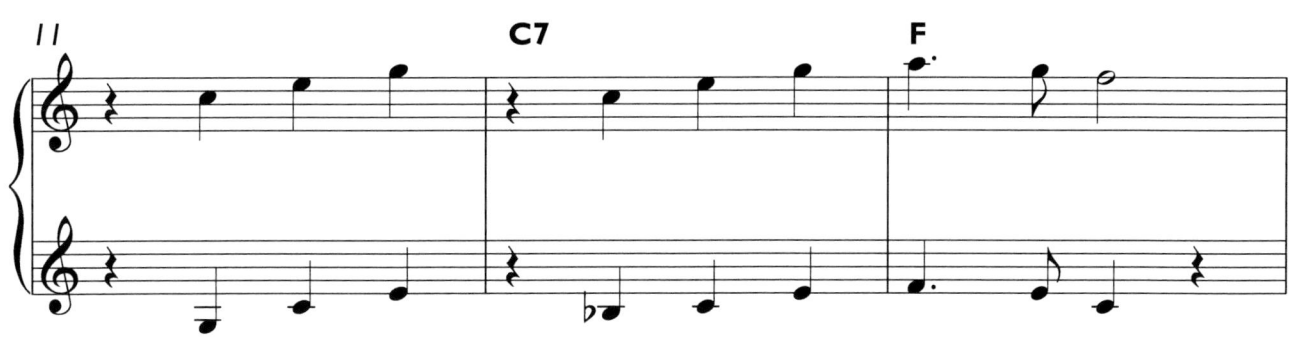

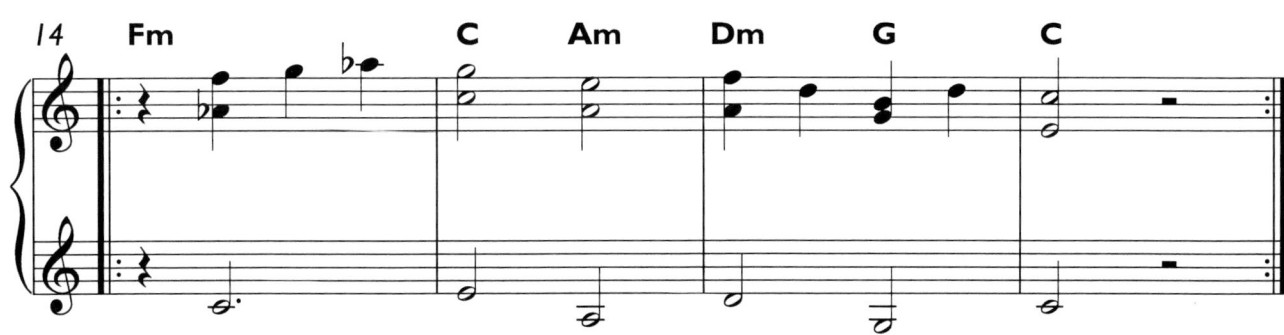

20. Merry-go-round

tuned percussion
(level 2)

Allegretto 124

counter melody
(level 2)

Allegretto 124

class music bumper pack
keyboard, counter melody and tuned percussion

20. Merry-go-round

keyboard
(level 2)

Allegretto 124

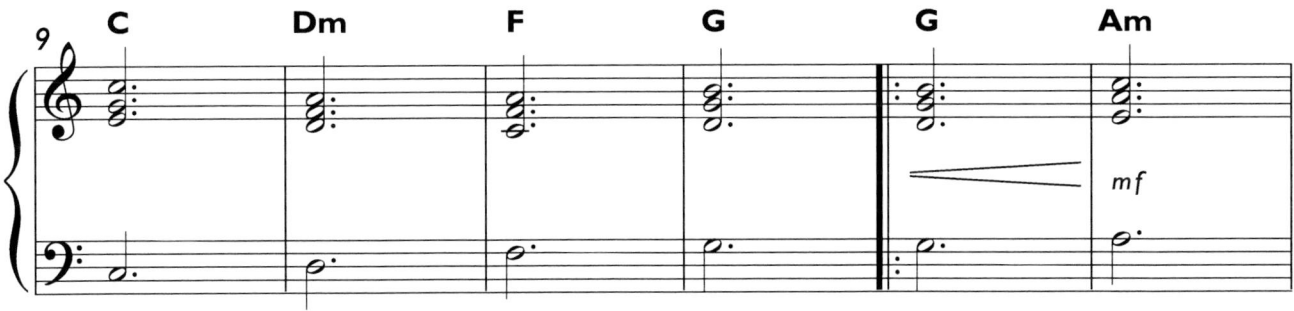

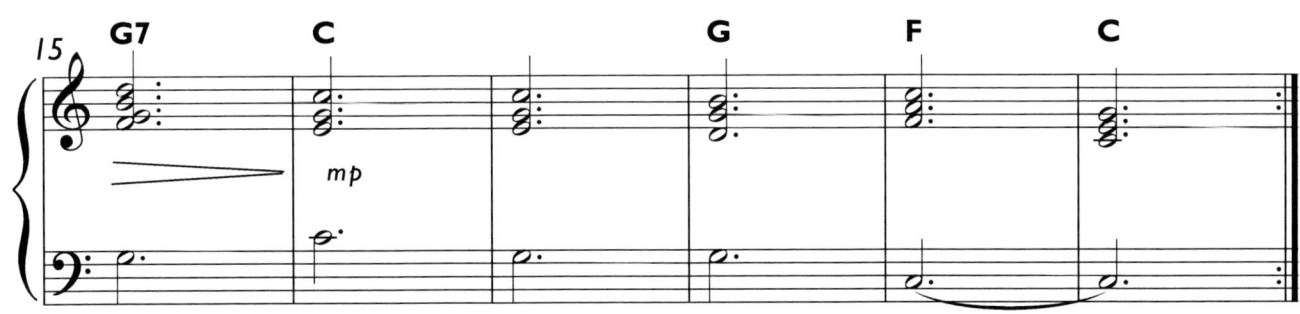

class music bumper pack
keyboard, counter melody and tuned percussion

21. Little Feet

Easy Feel 97

tuned percussion
(level 2)

D C# B A D C# B A

mf

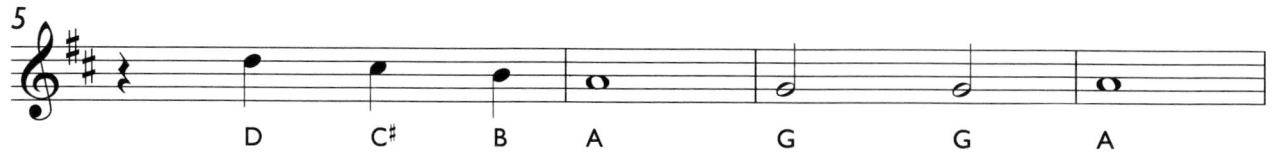

D C# B A G G A

D C# B A D C# B A

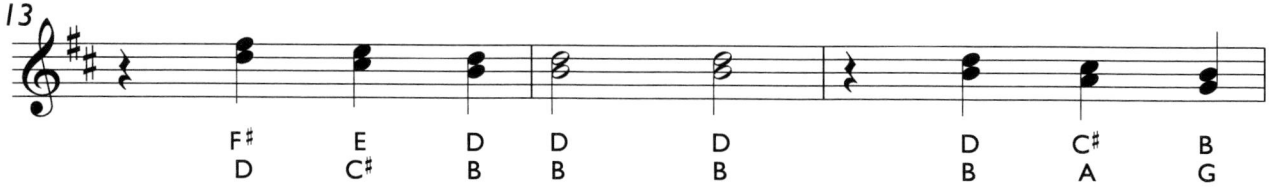

F# E D D D D C# B
D C# B B B B A G

A A D C# B
G G B A G

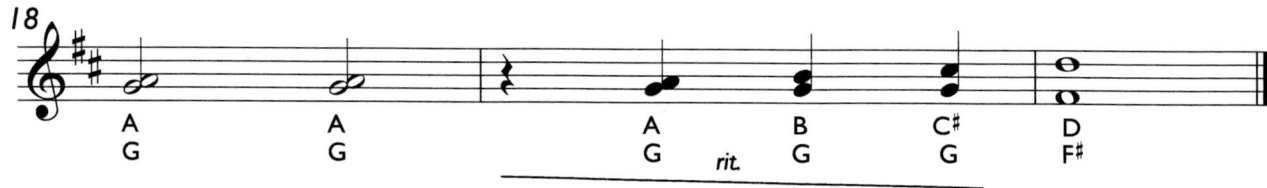

A A A B C# D
G G G G G F#
rit.

class music bumper pack
keyboard, counter melody and tuned percussion

21. Little Feet

keyboard
(level 2)

22. A Soldier's Tale

March Time 110

tuned percussion
(level 3)

class music bumper pack
keyboard, counter melody and tuned percussion

© Leckie & Leckie

22. A Soldier's Tale

March Time 110

22. A Soldier's Tale

keyboard
(level 2)

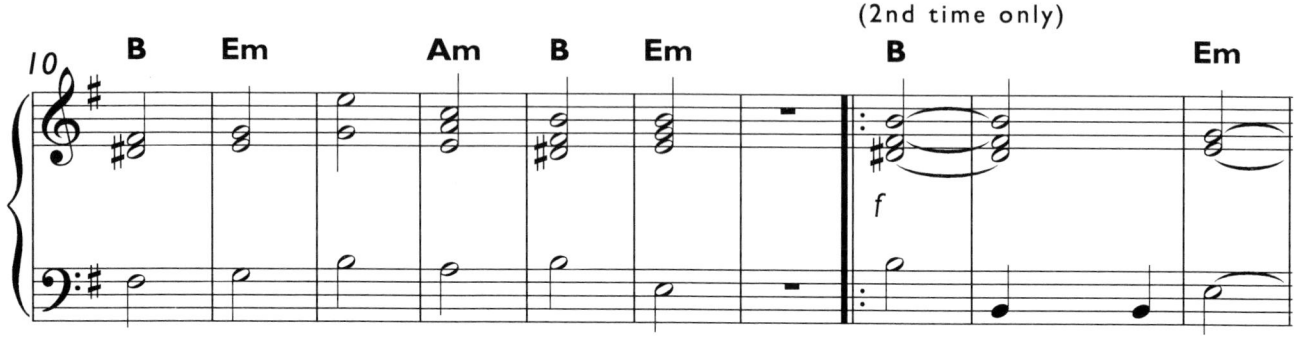

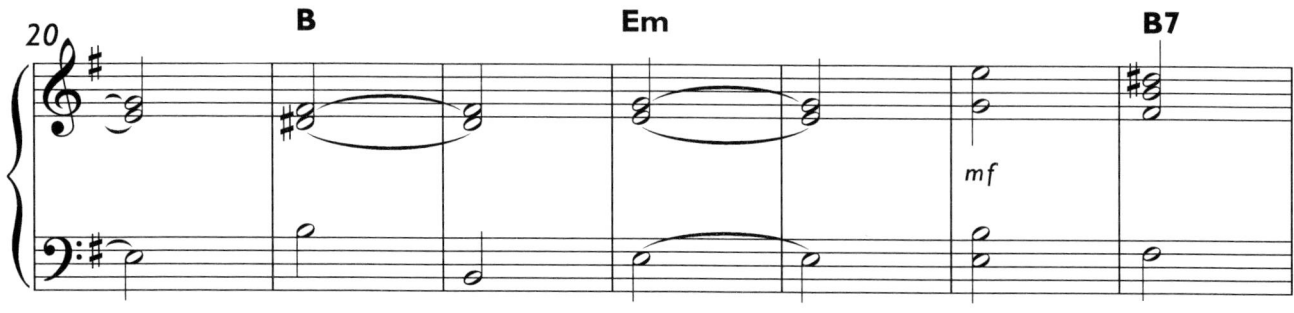

class music bumper pack
keyboard, counter melody and tuned percussion

23. Bodago Bay

tuned percussion
(level 2)

Latin Feel 124

class music bumper pack
keyboard, counter melody and tuned percussion

23. Bodago Bay

Latin Feel 124

class music bumper pack
keyboard, counter melody and tuned percussion

© Leckie & Leckie

23. Bodago Bay

keyboard
(level 3)

class music bumper pack
keyboard, counter melody and tuned percussion

63

24. Cowboy Boots

Country Style 105

class music bumper pack
keyboard, counter melody and tuned percussion

24. Cowboy Boots

Country Style 105

mf A A D F E D E F G E C C D C A

G C D E E E E F E C G A C A G G

A C A G F E f E G E A G

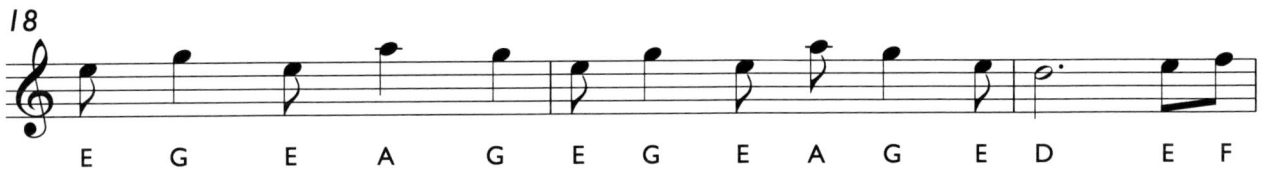

E G E A G E G E A G E D E F

G G G A G E C A C A G C D

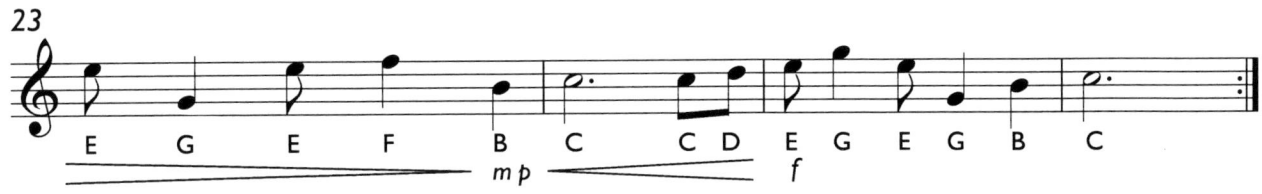

E G E F B C C D E G E G B C
mp f

24. Cowboy Boots

Country Style 105

class music bumper pack
keyboard, counter melody and tuned percussion

© Leckie & Leckie

25. Miss U

tuned percussion
(level 2)

Thoughtfully 90

class music bumper pack
keyboard, counter melody and tuned percussion

25. Miss U

Thoughtfully 90

class music bumper pack
keyboard, counter melody and tuned percussion

© Leckie & Leckie

25. Miss U

keyboard
(level 3)

Thoughtfully 90

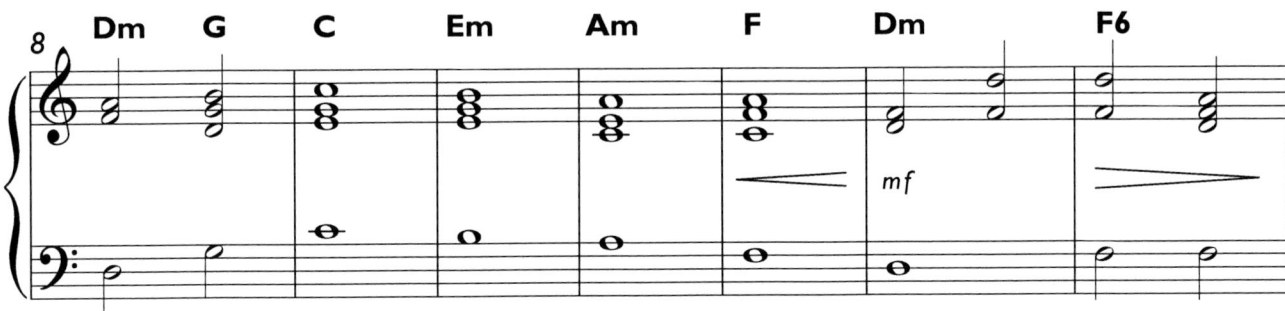

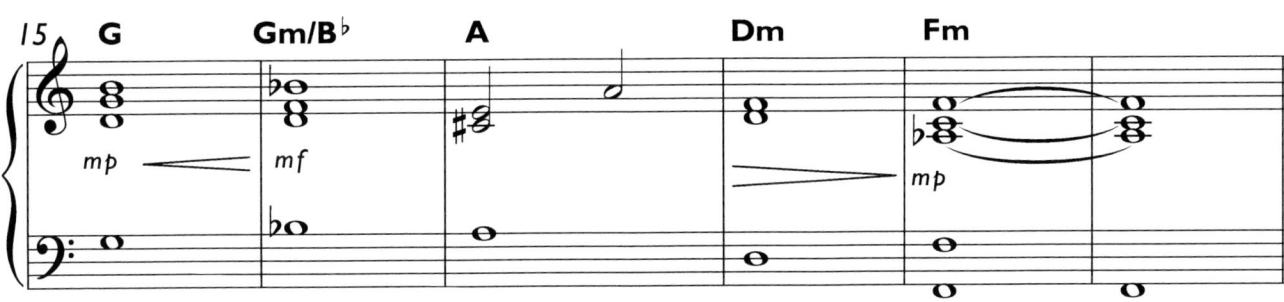

26. Irish Love Song

tuned percussion
(level 2)

Tempo Rubato 76

counter melody
(level 2)

Tempo Rubato 76

© Leckie & Leckie

26. Irish Love Song

keyboard
(level 2)

Tempo Rubato 76

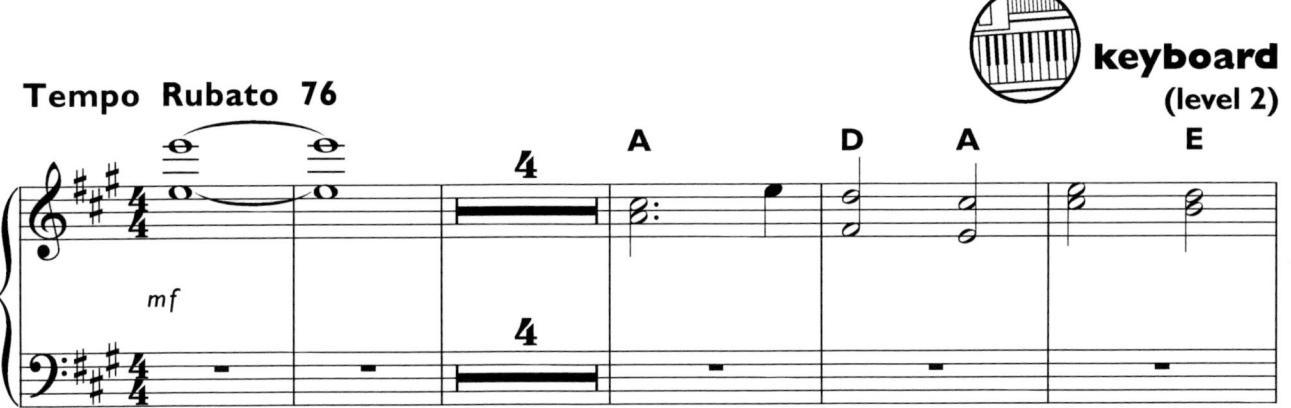

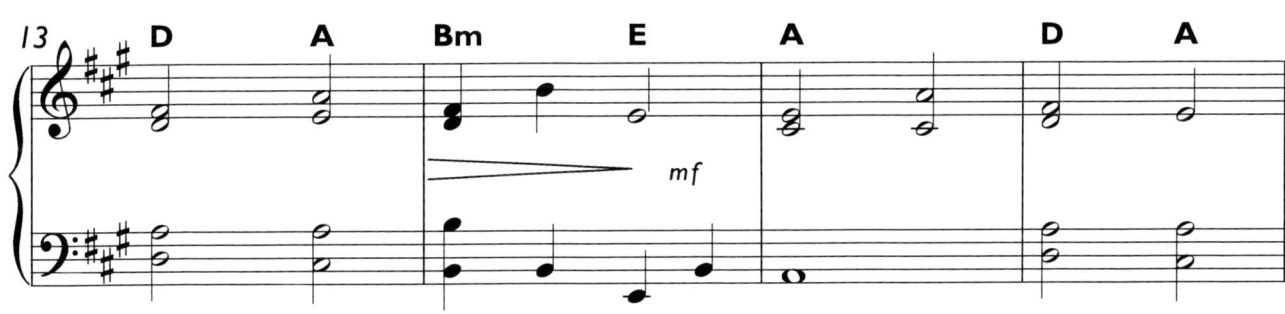

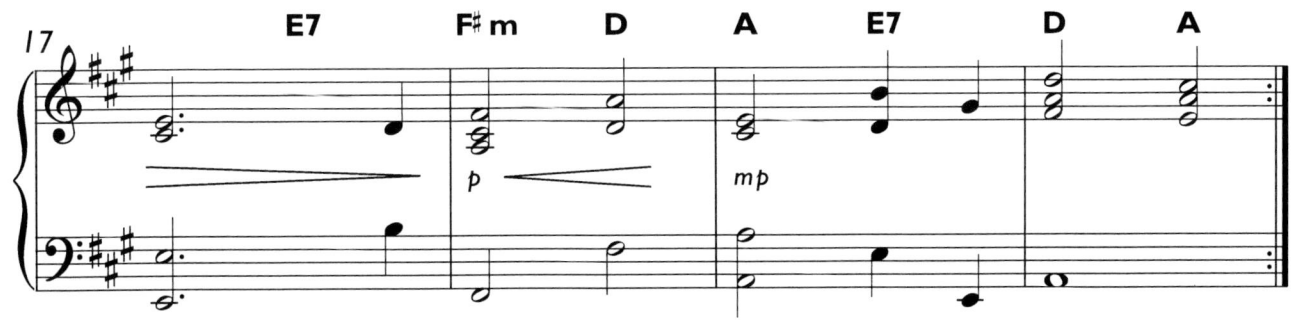

class music bumper pack
keyboard, counter melody and tuned percussion

27. Blue Denim

tuned percussion
(level 3)

Cool 106

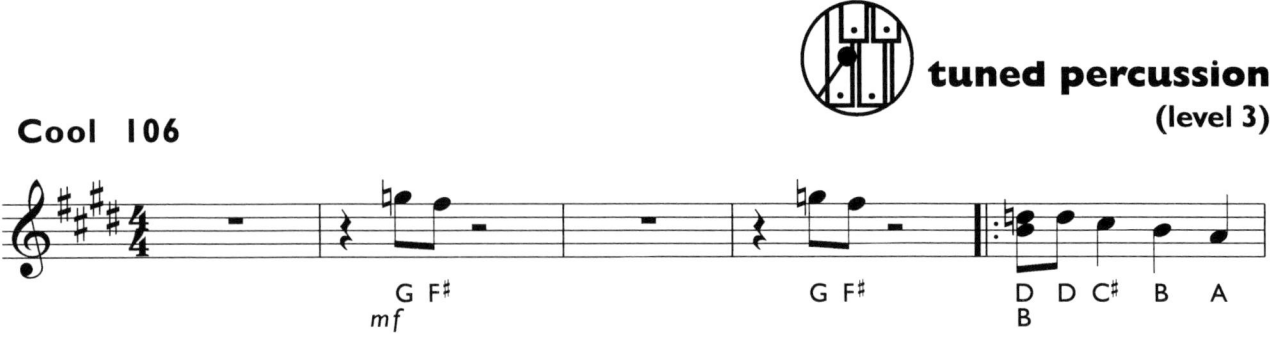

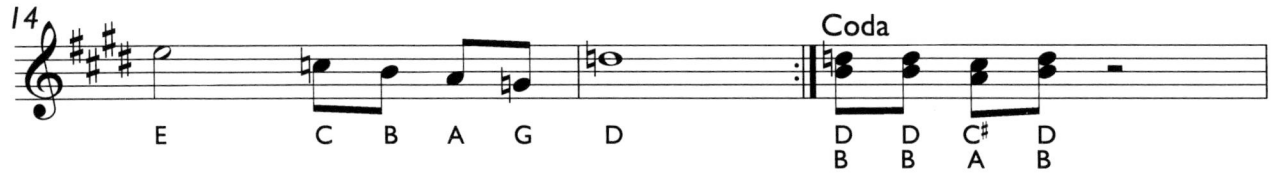

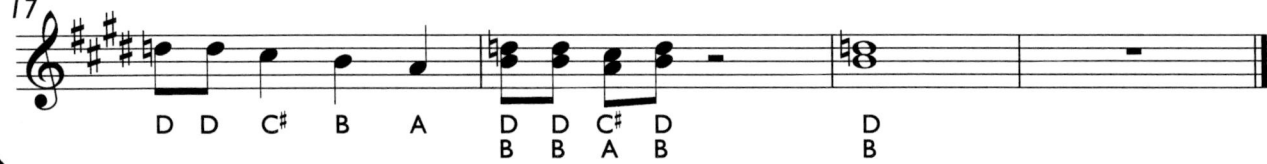

class music bumper pack
keyboard, counter melody and tuned percussion

27. Blue Denim

melody

includes counter melody instruments (level 3)

Cool 106

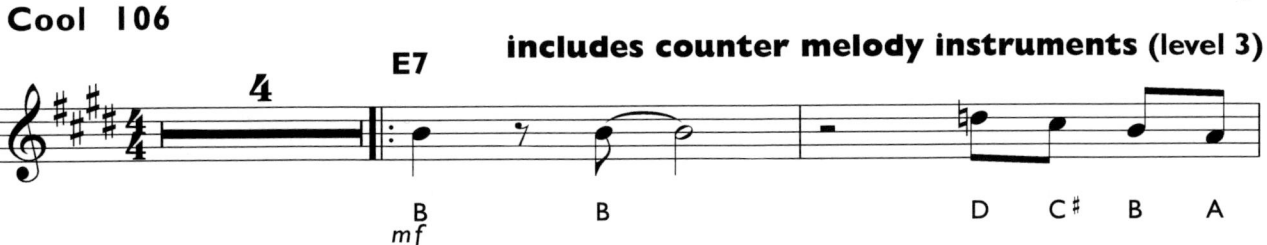

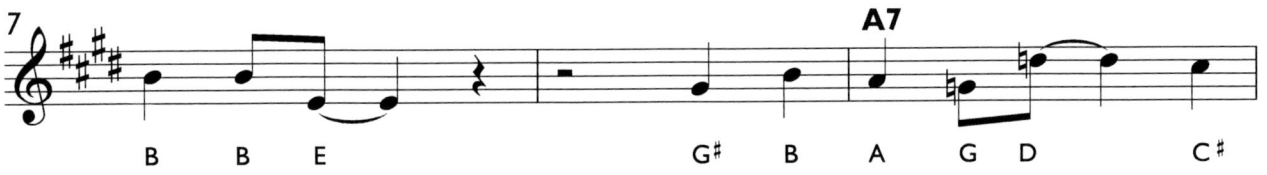

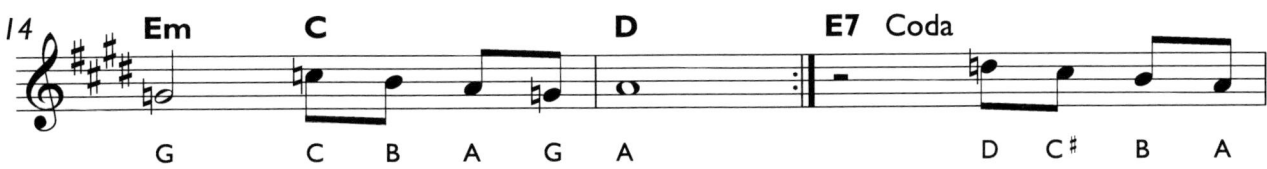

class music bumper pack
keyboard, counter melody and tuned percussion

27. Blue Denim

class music bumper pack
keyboard, counter melody and tuned percussion

28. Spanish Step

tuned percussion
(level 3)

Vivace 104

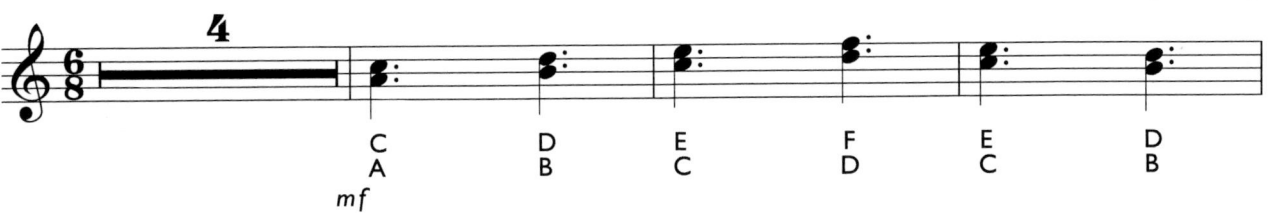

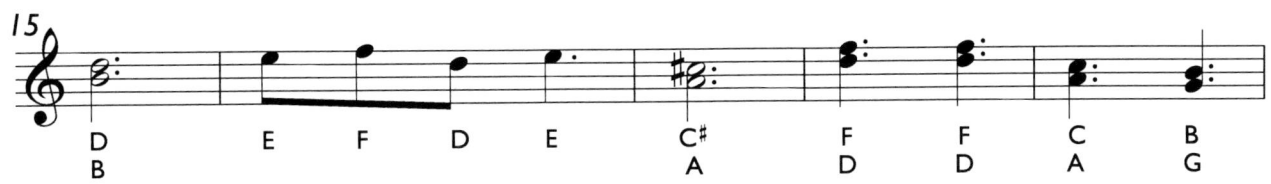

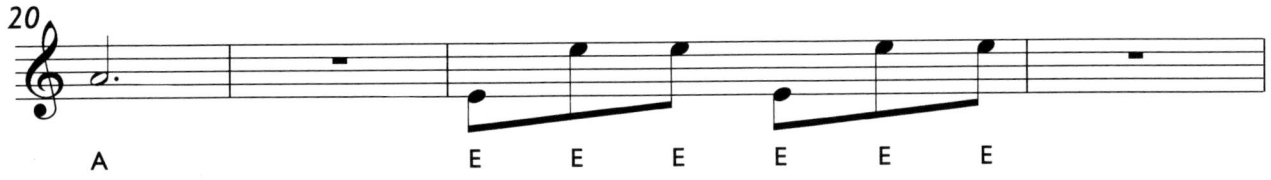

class music bumper pack
keyboard, counter melody and tuned percussion

 **tuned percussion (cont.)**

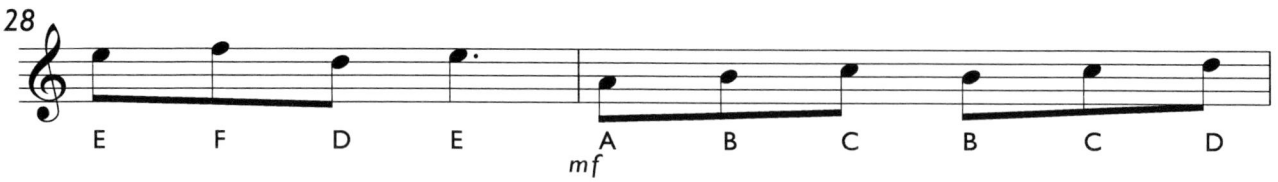

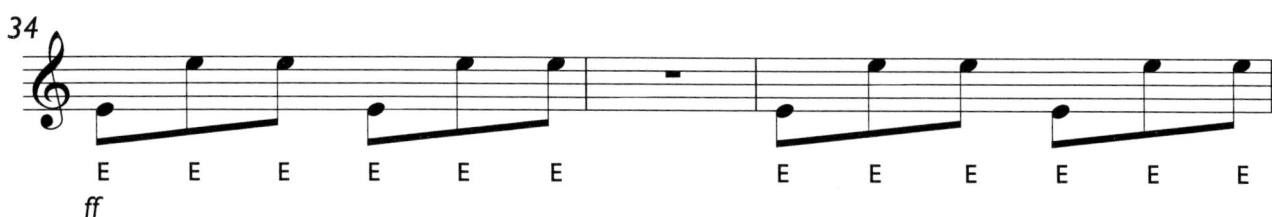

class music bumper pack
keyboard, counter melody and tuned percussion

28. Spanish Step

counter melody
(level 3)

Vivace   104

28. Spanish Step

keyboard
(level 4)

Vivace 104

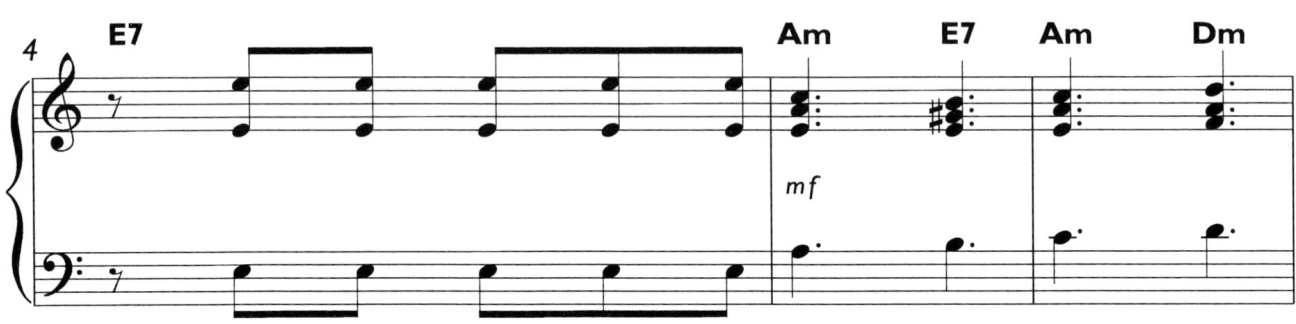

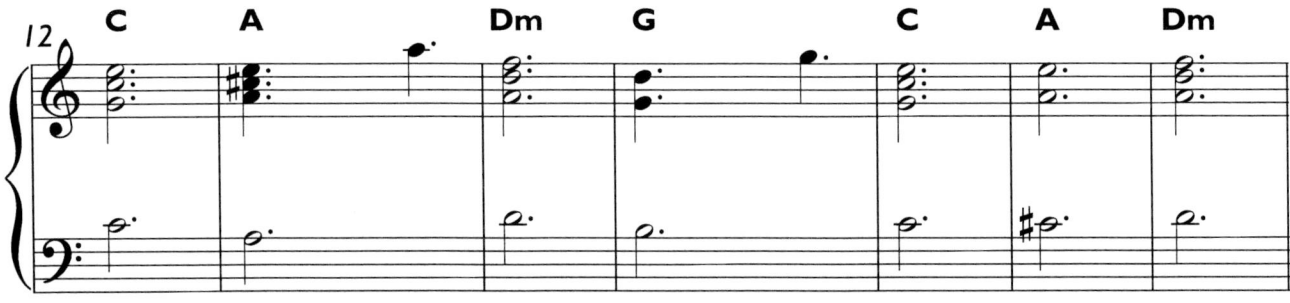

29. Ali's Back in Town

tuned percussion
(level 3)

Moderately 112

class music bumper pack
keyboard, counter melody and tuned percussion

29. Ali's Back in Town

counter melody
(level 3)

Moderately 112

class music bumper pack
keyboard, counter melody and tuned percussion

29. Ali's Back in Town

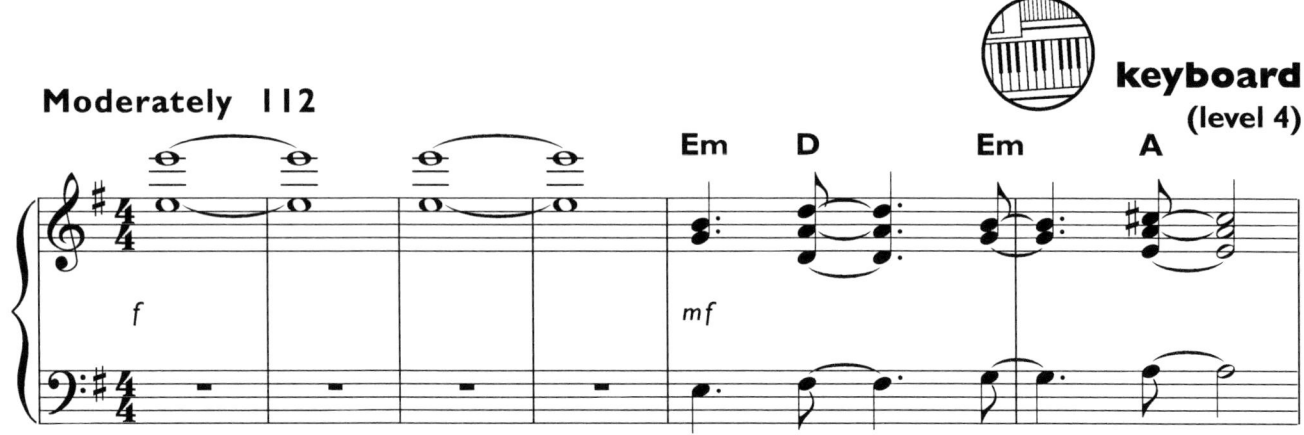

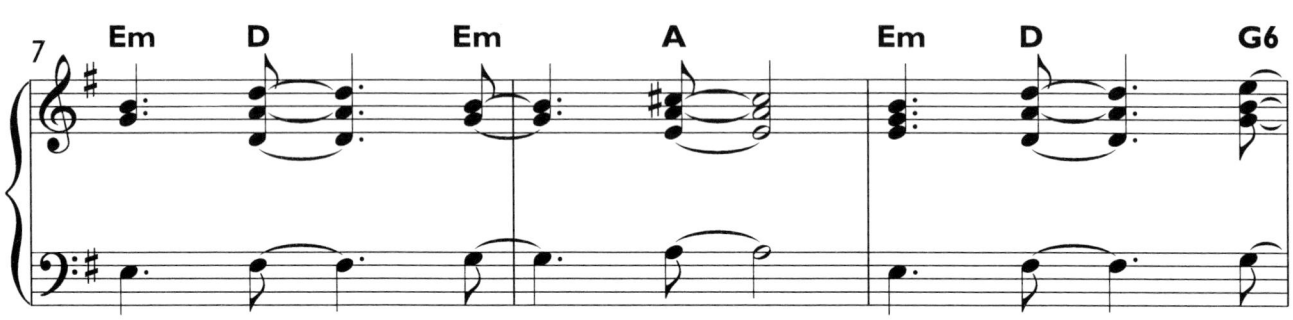

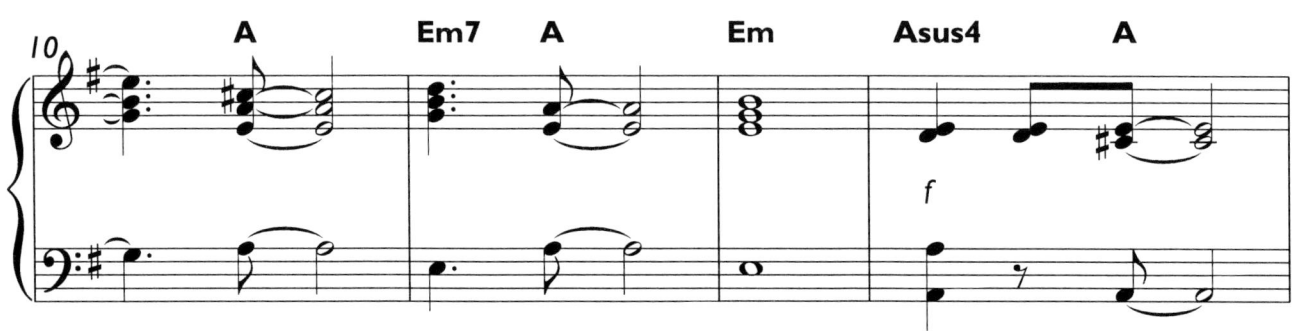

class music bumper pack
keyboard, counter melody and tuned percussion

keyboard (cont.)

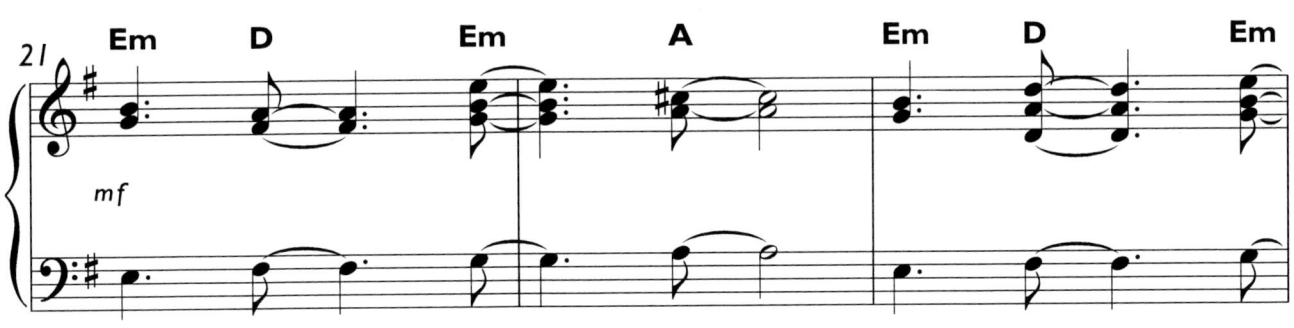

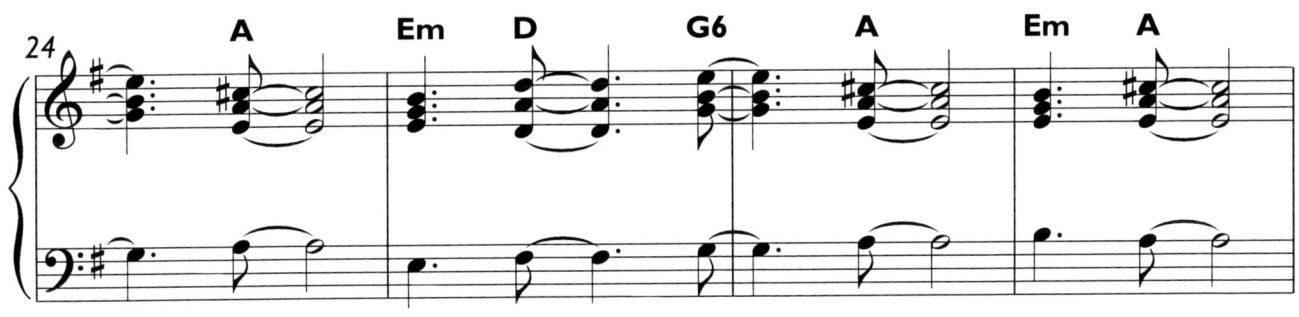

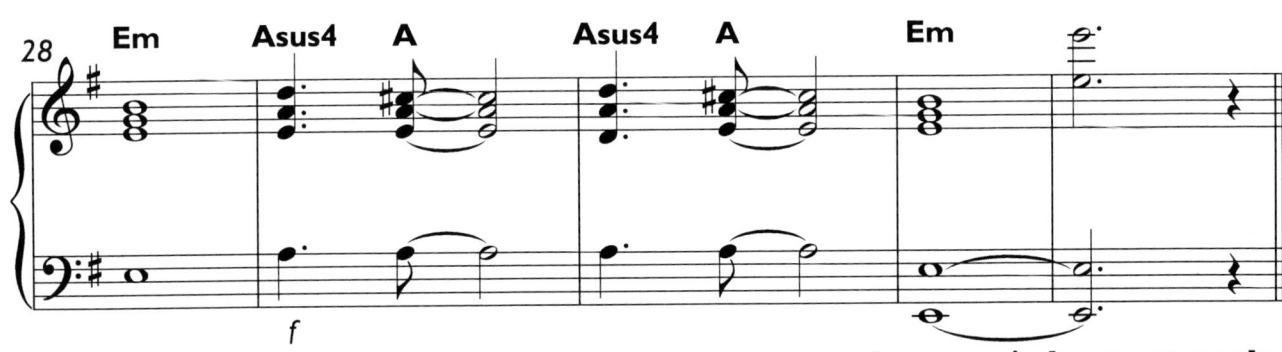

class music bumper pack **83**
keyboard, counter melody and tuned percussion

30. Mayfield Rag

Rag Swing 110

tuned percussion
(level 3)

class music bumper pack
keyboard, counter melody and tuned percussion

© Leckie & Leckie

30. Mayfield Rag

Rag Swing 110

class music bumper pack
keyboard, counter melody and tuned percussion

85

30. Mayfield Rag

Rag Swing 110

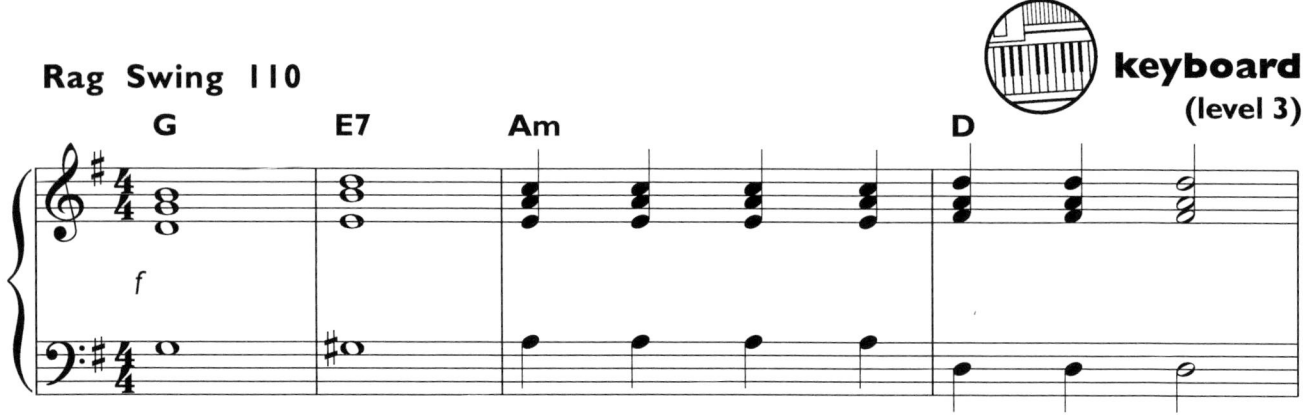

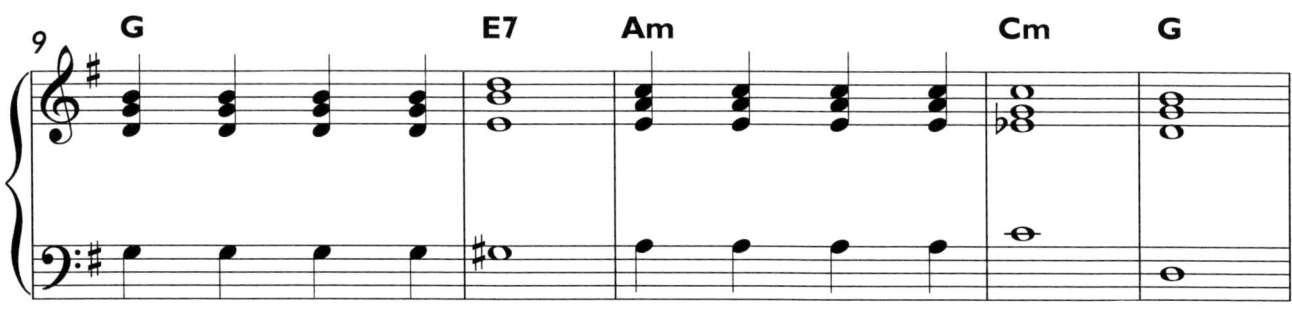

class music bumper pack
keyboard, counter melody and tuned percussion

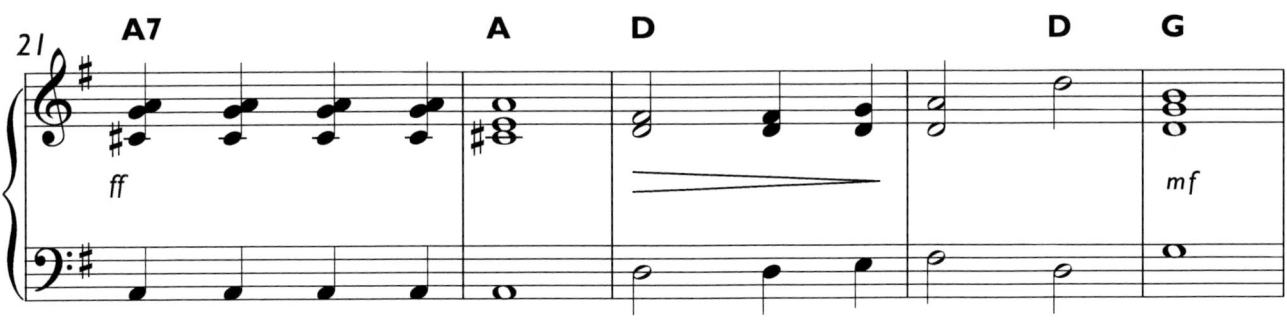

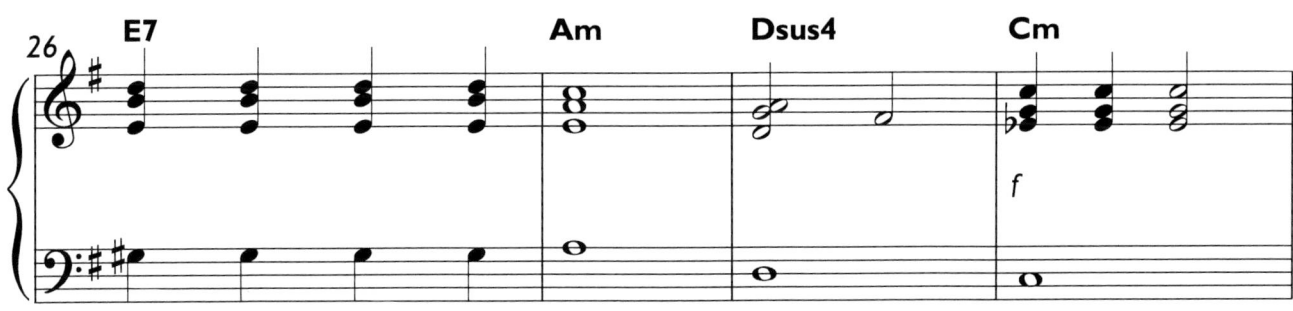

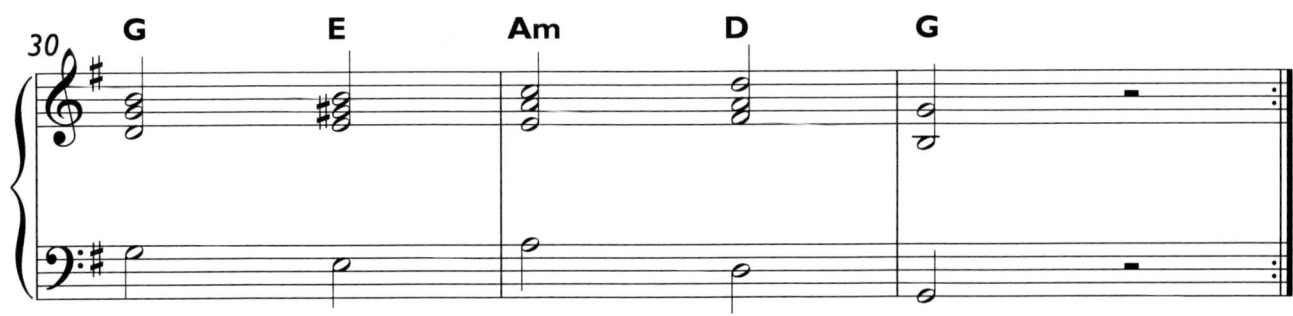

class music bumper pack

keyboard, counter melody and tuned percussion

More Leckie & Leckie Music Titles for 1999–2000

Class Music Guitar Melody Book with CD
Strive for six-string success with this impressive collection of 30 progressive melodies for the young guitarist. The 30 track CD provides backing tracks to help you towards GCSE/Standard Grade and beyond.

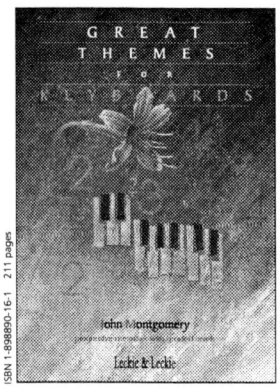

Great Themes for Keyboards
30 classic melodies, from Mozart to Abba and many original themes written for the progressing keyboard player. Each piece has suggested levels for exams, and tips to improve your playing.

Standard Grade Music Course Notes with CD
This is the only book of its kind available, so if you're a music student, it's a must! But we've made sure you get everything you need and much more. The 30 track CD will entertain and inspire!

Drums Live with CDs
Strike a lively tempo with this percussion book-and-CD package. Learn your way around the kit, as you progress from basic rhythms to more complex pieces aimed at GCSE/Standard Grade.

Once Upon a Castle – An Adventure Musical
Piano/Vocal score
From the dungeons of Edinburgh Castle, come with us on a magical journey through time. This musical is packed with memorable songs and a variety of 14 main parts, plus full chorus. Instrument parts/librettos available for hire.

Deacon Brodie – A Music Theatre Presentation
Piano/Vocal score
Enthralling, real-life story of an eighteenth-century rogue. This script with original music score has been highly praised. Instrument parts/librettos available for hire.
'Excellent musical' *The Scotsman*

More music products coming online soon! Check our website for new titles. For your updated Leckie & Leckie catalogue and further information about new music books and CDs, please contact us at:

Leckie & Leckie®
P U B L I S H E R S

8 Whitehill Terrace
St. Andrews, Scotland KY16 8RN
tel: 01334 475656
fax: 01334 477392
email: hq@leckieandleckie.com
web: www.leckieandleckie.com